CAPITALISTS WITHOUT CAPITALISM

CONTRIBUTIONS IN SOCIOLOGY

Series Editor: Don Martindale

CONTRIBUTIONS IN SOCIOLOGY, NUMBER 6

CAPITALISTS WITHOUT CAPITALISM

The Jains of India and the Quakers of the West

BALWANT NEVASKAR

GREENWOOD PUBLISHING CORPORATION
WESTPORT, CONNECTICUT

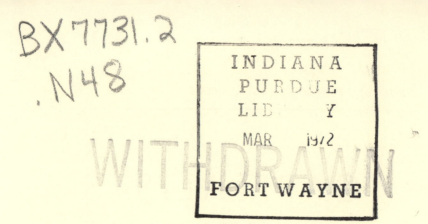
Acknowledgment is given to the publishers listed below
for permission to reprint from the books cited:
Charles Scribner's Sons and George Allen & Unwin, Ltd., for *The
Protestant Ethic and the Spirit of Capitalism* by Max Weber,
translated by Talcott Parsons.
William B. Eerdmans Publishing Company for *The Rich Heritage
of Quakerism* by Walter R. Williams.
Princeton University Press for *Philosophies of India*
by Heinrich Zimmer, edited by Joseph Campbell, Bollingen Series XXVI,
copyright 1951 by the Bollingen Foundation.
Van Nostrand Reinhold Company for *Social Life and Cultural Change*
by Don Martindale, copyright © by Litton Educational Publishing Inc.
The Macmillan Company for *Religion of India*
by Max Weber, translated by Hans H. Gerth and Don
Martindale, copyright © by The Free Press.

Library of Congress Catalog Card Number:72-98709
SBN: 8371-3297-5

Greenwood Publishing Corporation
51 Riverside Avenue, Westport, Connecticut 06880

Printed in the United States of America

FOR EDITH AND DON MARTINDALE

CONTENTS

FOREWORD

Two powerful currents flow through western social thought: holism and elementarism. Holism expresses the conviction that society and culture are realities per se such that they obey their own laws despite the preferences of individuals. Elementarism expresses the conviction that society and culture are never other than the activities of individuals and have only such order as individuals yield to them. Quite apart from the question whether these two perspectives are ultimately irreconcilable conceptualizations or merely differences of emphasis, the dialogue of their adherents has led to a fuller exploration of social life than could have been anticipated had either occupied the field alone. In a few instances, problems posed from the standpoint of one perspective have been taken up and pursued further from the standpoint of the other. Such is the case with a tradition extending from Max Weber to which the present study belongs.

The idealistic social philosophy of Hegel was holistic,

monistic, and dedicated to the doctrine of progress. Man's sociocultural life was conceived as an entity. Man's collective social psychology (his spirit) was conceived as the mainspring of history. His sociocultural life, conceived as a unitary phenomenon, was thought to develop cyclically in a progressive manner toward ever increasing self-realization. In Hegel's words:

> In the history of the World, the *Individuals* we have to do with are *Peoples*. . . . Universal History . . . belongs to the realm of *Spirit*. The term *"World"* includes both physical and psychical Nature. . . . But Spirit, and the course of its development, is our substantial object. . . . The History of the world is none other than the progress of the consciousness of Freedom. . . . The Eastern nations knew only that *one* is free; the Greek and Roman world only that *some* are free; while *we* know that all men absolutely (man *as man*) are free. . . . *The final cause of the World at large,* we allege, to be the consciousness of its own freedom on the part of Spirit.[1]

Karl Marx took over the holism, monism, and progress doctrine of Hegel into his own system. However, classes rather than nations were viewed as the true individual agents of history. In place of man's collective psychology (his spirit), the relations of material production were conceived as the mainspring of history. In place of an autonomous state of world self-realization, a world socialistic epoch was conceived as the fulfillment of history. In his *A Contribution to the Critique of Political Economy,* Karl Marx formulated his theory of history:

> In the social production which men carry on they enter into definite relations that are indispensable and independent of their will; these relations of production correspond to a

definite stage of development of their material powers of production. The sum total of these relations of production constitutes the economic structure of society—the real foundation, on which rise legal and political superstructures and to which correspond definite forms of social consciousness. The mode of production in material life determines the general character of the social, political, and spiritual processes of life. It is not the consciousness of men that determines their existence, but, on the contrary, their social existence determines their consciousness. At a certain stage of their development the material forces of production in society come into conflict with the existing relations of production. . . . From forms of development of the forces of production these relations turn into their fetters. Then comes the period of social revolution. With the change of the economic foundation the entire immense superstructure is more or less rapidly transformed. . . . No social order ever disappears before all the productive forces for which there is room in it have been developed. . . . Therefore mankind always takes up only such problems as it can solve. . . . In broad outlines we can designate the Asiatic, the ancient, the feudal, and the modern bourgeois methods of production as so many epochs in the progress of the economic formation of society. The bourgeois relations of production are the last antagonistic form of the social process of production. . . . At the same time the productive forces developing in the womb of bourgeois society create the material conditions for the solution of that antagonism. This social formation constitutes, therefore, the closing chapter of the prehistoric stage of human society.[2]

By treating the sociocultural life of an epoch as a unitary entity, holists of both idealistic and materialistic persuasions subscribed to the hypothesis that all aspects of the sociocultural life of a period are interrelated. Their monism forced them to seek a primary source of this interrelation. The

Hegelians and Marxians were, thus, brought into direct confrontation. For Hegel all stylization of social life proceeds out of religion.

> The State is the actually existing, realized moral life. . . .
> The State is the Divine Idea as it exists on Earth. . . .
> Religion stands in the closest connection with the political principle. Freedom can exist only where Individuality is recognized as having its positive and real existence in the Divine Being.[3]

For Marx, morality and religion are a mere superstructure resting on material life processes.

> The phantoms formed in the human brain are also, necessarily, sublimates of their material life process, which is empirically verifiable and bound to material premises. Morality, religion, metaphysics, all the rest of ideology and their corresponding forms of consciousness, thus no longer retain the semblance of independence. They have no history, no development; but men, developing their material production and their material intercourse, alter, along with this, their real existence, their thinking, and the products of their thinking.[4]

Since two of the most influential holistic traditions of the nineteenth century thus posed the problem of the interrelations between religious and economic life and came to opposite conclusions about it, it was perhaps inevitable that adherents of the elementaristic positions that arose toward the end of the nineteenth and early twentieth centuries should have been encouraged to try their hand at the solution of the problem.

Among the major ways in which the elementarist differs from the holist are: in his reluctance to view society as an entity; in his preference for viewing society as a loosely integrated set of strategies of various social groups; in his view that all forms of social and cultural life arise only as the activities of individuals and pluralities; in his view that the individual cannot be dismissed as unimportant.

Very direct consequences for the concept of sociocultural interrelations flow from the elementarist conception of society as a set of strategies of pluralities. There is no longer an a priori reason why all aspects of a given sociocultural epoch should form a single system of interrelated phenomena. There is good reason to believe that they will not. While the strategy of collective action of one group may bind a variety of cultural phenomena into a single complex, the strategy of another group may not. For example, the religious and economic concerns of one group may form a close-knit system; the religious and economic concerns of another group in the same society may be for all intents and purposes unrelated. This does not mean that for the elementarist there are no interrelations between one aspect of society and another, but that many possible kinds and degrees of interrelation must be anticipated.

The monocausal hypothesis and closely related notion that social change is dialectical also come under fire from an elementaristic perspective. Holistic notions of sociocultural life appear always to press their adherents toward monistic notions of social causation. The idea that society is a unique entity suggests that a single informing principle establishes its nature. Moreover, if this entity is assumed to undergo change primarily from forces arising within itself, the notion of an antagonism between its informing principle and some counterforce which it overcomes (a dialectic) in a spiral of progressive development is an attractive possibility. However, if one believes that sociocultural events do not constitute an entity at all, but are at best the complex accommodation and clash of the strategies of a variety of groups, society has no single informing principle. The elementarist is convinced that there are always many groups. They are moved by a variety of interests and operate with a wide range of techniques and at varied rates.

When Max Weber took up the problem of the relation between the rise of the capitalistic economic system and a set of attitudes and beliefs which he felt to be widely distributed through Christendom and intensified in some of the Protestant sects, he was widely interpreted to have entered the conflict between the idealistic and materialistic social philosophers. However, the concept that *The Protestant Ethic* is an answer to Marx rather thoroughly distorts its significance. Weber did maintain that the notion of historical materialism—the moral and religious ideas of man represent a mere reflection or superstructure of economic conditions—is naive.[5] In fact, he observes, ideas and attitudes which we have come to think of as typical of the contemporary entrepreneur were almost completely absent from Florence of the fourteenth and fifteenth centuries, though it was the most highly developed capitalistic center of the time. These ideas and attitudes were characteristic of the small bourgeois of Pennsylvania in the eighteenth century where the sheer lack of money constantly threatened to turn business into a bartering operation and where there were no large enterprises but only the rudiments of a banking system. Weber observes: "To speak here of a reflection of material conditions in the ideal superstructure would be patent nonsense." [6]

While Weber established beyond any question that re-

ligious forces, which appear in full clarity in some phases of
the Reformation, played a part in the qualitative formation
and quantitative expansion of the psychology of capitalism,
he emphatically denied that one could explain the Reformation on the basis of economic factors alone or that the "spirit
of capitalism . . . could only have arisen as a result of
certain effects of the Reformation, or even that capitalism
as an economic system is a creation of the Reformation." [7]
In this connection Weber observed that many important features of capitalistic business organization are considerably
older than the Reformation.

However, while Weber emphatically rejected the treatment
of religious attitudes and beliefs as mere reflections or superstructure of economic relations, he was also unwilling to
subscribe to the notion that economic institutions have no
influence on religious attitudes and beliefs. While his specific
object had been to trace various economic consequences of
ascetic rationalism developed in religious contexts, he also
observed that the study also indicated "how Protestant
Asceticism was in turn influenced in its development and its
character by the totality of social conditions, especially economic." Weber concluded: "It is, of course, not my aim to
substitute for a one-sided materialistic an equally one-sided
spiritualistic causal interpretation of culture and of history." [8]

Thus it is a mistake to view Max Weber's *The Protestant
Ethic* as an attempt to refute Marx. So far as he was refuting
anything it was the monocausal hypotheses, whether it be
spiritualistic or materialistic. So far as he was advocating
anything it was a pluralistic analysis of sociocultural causation.
However, Weber does not seem to have been primarily inclined either to refute or to advocate, but to explore some

of the complex interrelations that appeared to exist between religious attitudes and beliefs and a type of psychology peculiar to high capitalism.

While Max Weber's *The Protestant Ethic* self-consciously took issue with the monocausal hypotheses of the nineteenth-century holists, he implicitly took issue with their holism as well. In seeking the origins of the psychology of the bearers of high capitalism, Weber found it to be present in more or less pure forms first among particular groups whose ascetic rationalism began to interact with the forms of their economic enterprise. When the linkage proved to be successful and a way of life began to develop under its impetus, the complex diffused from its points of origin until it increasingly came to dominate major sectors of the Western world. This has direct implications for the theory of social change, for it would indicate that the development of high capitalism did not take its point of departure from the whole nor take the form of a dialectical development, but occurred in the form of a diffusion to other groups of a strategy originating in particular groups.

Professor Nevaskar's investigation of the religious ethic and practical economic conduct of the Quakers in America and the Jains of India illustrates the continuing value of the type of analysis Max Weber undertook in his classical study of the Protestant ethic and spirit of capitalism. In his study *The Religion of India,* Weber has called attention to some similarities between the two socioreligious developments:

> In substance, the commandments of Jain asceticism . . . placed supreme importance on *ahimsa,* the absolute prohibition of the killing . . . of living beings. . . . The practice of *ahimsa* led to the exclusion of the Jain from all

industrial trades endangering life. . . . The second most important commandment for the laity was the limitation of possessions. . . . As with Protestantism, "joy in possessions" . . . was the objectionable thing, but not possession or gain in itself. The similarity extends further: a Jain commandment forbids saying anything false or exaggerated; the Jains believed in absolute honesty in business life, all deception . . . was prohibited, including . . . all dishonest gain through smuggling, bribery and . . . disreputable financial practice. . . . This excluded the sect . . . from typical oriental participation in "political capitalism" (accumulation of wealth by officials, tax farmers, state purveyors) and . . . it worked among them . . . as for the Quakers in the Occident, in terms of the dictum . . . "honesty is the best policy." The honesty of the Jain trader was famous. Their wealth was also famous: formerly it has been maintained that more than half the trade of India passed through their hands.[9]

Professor Nevaskar's extended investigation powerfully confirms Max Weber's intuition that parallels between Jain and Quaker religious beliefs were correlated with parallels in their everyday economic practices. Pacifism, asceticism, and an ethic of honesty and fair dealing were parallel religiously based beliefs of both Jain and Quaker. This inclined members of both groups to shun occupations offensive to their pacifism: both shunned political and military careers as well as certain types of industrial and agricultural pursuits. Urban and commercial pursuits, particularly the retail trade, appear in both cases to have supplied one of the few ways of making a living consistent with religious requirements. The religious ethic of both groups appears to have played a major role in their financial and commercial successes. In both cases strict religious prohibitions were opposed to the expenditure of wealth on display or other forms of self-indulgence. Members of both Jain and Quaker communities are notable for the use of their wealth for reinvestment in business and for acts of charity. In the case of neither is it necessary to assume that their religiosity was exclusively caused by their economic practices or their economic practices exclusively caused by their religiosity. However, that these two components of their life styles were linked stands beyond any question. This linkage appears to have developed in a spiral of mutual reinforcement over time, increasing the solidarity and effectiveness of the respective subgroups within the context of their wider societies.

The implications for the holistic hypothesis (whether it be advocated by adherents of early nineteenth-century Absolute Idealism, Historical Materialism, or contemporary Structure-Functionalism) is clear. It is possible for close affinities to develop between the religious beliefs and economic practices of subgroups of a society, affinities which provide this subgroup with special survival value. Such a linkage is possible not only when it is more or less in accord with the system of social practice of the wider society as in the case of Quakerism in the West, but when it has no close relation to the system of social practice or the wider society as in the case of Jainism in India.

This finding calls into question the notion that society is a functionally interrelated unit that in the long run can sustain only a single dominant value system. It calls into question the notion that sociocultural development necessarily proceeds from tensions within the whole and that social change always assumes a dialectical form. It opens the question as to how far the sociocultural practices of subgroups can diverge from the practice of the wider society without precipitating conflict. It opens the question whether general laws can be established with regard to the circumstances when the practices of sub-groups may either be curtailed by those of the wider society or may spread beyond their spheres of origin and become general to the wider society.

Professor Nevaskar's study establishes the Quakers of America and the Jains of India as specialized subgroups who developed reciprocal systems of religious beliefs and economic practices providing each with a tough internal unity able to resist full incorporation into their wider societies. The Quakers have sustained a record paralleled by few other groups of reformist activity. In their elaboration of pacifism as a way of life they have, for three hundred years, preferred to suffer various forms of persecution rather than take up arms. For more than a millennium the Jains have managed to resist full incorporation into the Indian caste system and have elaborated a system of economic practice in many ways closer to that of the West than to that of the Orient. There seems little doubt that, in each case, it has been the interrelation of religious and everyday ethic and practice that has permitted the Quakers to retain the image of pacifistic ascetics in a materialistic world, and the Jains the image of capitalists in a world without capitalism.

Don Martindale

NOTES

1. Georg Wilhelm Friedrich Hegel, *The Philosophy of History*, trans. J. Sibree (New York: Wiley Book Co., 1944), pp. 14, 16, 19.

2. Karl Marx, *A Contribution to the Critique of Political Economy,* trans. from the second German edition by N. I. Stone (Chicago: Charles H. Kerr, 1904), pp. 11, 12.

3. Hegel, *The Philosophy of History,* pp. 38, 39, 50.

4. Karl Marx and Friedrich Engels, *The German Ideology,* ed. R. Pascal (London: Lawrence and Wishart, 1939), p. 5.

5. Max Weber. *The Protestant Ethic and the Spirit of Capitalism,* trans. Talcott Parsons (New York: Charles Scribner's Sons, 1930), p. 55.

6. Ibid., p. 75.

7. Ibid., p. 91.

8. Ibid., p. 183.

9. Max Weber, *The Religion of India,* trans. Hans H. Gerth and Don Martindale (Glencoe, Ill.: The Free Press, 1958), pp. 198, 199, 120.

PREFACE

In 1904, the *Archiv Fur Sozialwissenschaft* published
Max Weber's *The Protestant Ethic and the Spirit of Capitalism* and set off one of the great debates in recent Western
thought. The reasons for the dramatic reception of Weber's
essay was that Weber was the first Western thinker to show
effectively the influence of religious sentiments on everyday
practices, particularly economic behavior.

Weber wrote at the end of the nineteenth century when the
economics of Western nations were dominated by the institutions of laissez-faire capitalism. As yet, there was no serious
competition to capitalism from socialistic economic activities.
Weber assumed that an important task of social science was to
explain why capitalism in its Western form had arisen solely
in the Occident.

At the time Weber was writing, an interest in the origins
of capitalism was vigorously being pursued by intellectuals of
socialistic persuasion, particularly by followers of Marxism.

The Marxians, however, phrased the problem differently. They took the "bull by the horns," so to speak, and instead of asking how any particular economy arose out of its conditions, they assumed that the economy was causally prior to those conditions. Their problem, thus, was solved by a tour de force: for them the only task remaining was to specify the mechanisms by which socioeconomic development was accomplished. These mechanisms, as is well known, consisted of a sequence of class struggles resulting from conflicts of interest between producers and possessors. Moreover, consistent with the assumption of the primacy of economics, Marxists and other scientific socialists visualized all other social phenomena as mere extensions of economic concern. Marx, for example, dismissed religion as being the opiate of the masses that served to obfuscate their pursuit of their socioeconomic heritage.

Many thinking persons in the nineteenth century were not satisfied with the explanations given by Marx and the scientific socialists for either the rise of capitalism or the relation between capitalistic economic institutions and other cultural institutions. Such dissatisfaction stemmed not merely from conservative inclinations, but from scientific and scholarly reasons.

Anyone acquainted with the social experience of mankind can draw examples of numerous occasions when people apparently have acted for noneconomic reasons. How can one assign economic motives to a soldier who dies on the battlefield for his country? What is his economic profit? How can one assign economic motives to the behavior of a wealthy man who gives his fortune to charity and enters a religious establishment? How can one assign economic motives to a person who donates his wealth to educational philanthropies or the promotion of the arts? The further one ranges through human experience, the more one becomes aware of the many examples in which the reduction of behavior to economic explanation distorts its meaning in a fundamental sense.

If one accepts the position that there are many categories of social behavior incapable of reduction to direct or indirect economic form, one cannot accept the unquestioned premise of Marxism as to the primacy of economic behavior. Some of the great events in the West associated with the rise of capitalism fall outside of the Marxian explanation.

Having arrived at this position, Weber reflected that economic behavior is not always primary. The Marxian account of the rise of capitalism was seen to be incomplete and Weber realized that it was necessary to undertake a new explanation for the rise of capitalism. History proved that at many times and places in the world, the essential economic conditions for capitalism had been present before they appeared in the recent West; however, capitalism itself never developed. Weber, thus, realized that it was essential to assign greater weight to the noneconomic phenomena. He primarily attempted to explain the peculiar psychology which was always central to capitalistic economic behavior in its early period. Furthermore, since most peoples' sociopsychological outlooks are closely related to their religious orientation, Weber proposed the bold hypothesis that in the rise of capitalism, Western man's religion, far from serving merely as a reactionary support of the status quo, played a dramatically central role in the generation of capitalism's revolutionary psychology. With *The Protestant Ethic and the Spirit of Capitalism,* one of the most exciting intellectual debates of the twentieth century was launched.

Weber's theories have been modified in the course of these

discussions, but his primary formulations have been retained in substance. The present study was conceived in the tradition of these debates concerning the role of religion and socioeconomic behavior. Its purpose is to trace, on a cross-cultural basis, the relationship between the religion and socioeconomic behavior of the Quakers of America and the Jains of India. The discussion will take the following general form: first, an examination of Weber's hypothesis and some of the major modifications to which it has been subjected; second, a presentation of Quaker institutions and ethic, and an examination of the application of this ethic to everyday life including economic behavior; third, a parallel presentation of the histories and ethic and application of this ethic by Jainism; and finally, a comparison of the two developments.

The hypothesis that will be explored in the following study is that the relation of the socioeconomic ethic to everyday conduct is especially significant because it may produce results which contradict other major influences in the environment. If this hypothesis holds true, it strongly contradicts contemporary theories that attempt to explain socioeconomic behavior solely in terms of the prevailing social milieu.

ACKNOWLEDGMENTS

It is impossible for me to acknowledge adequately my indebtedness to the many colleagues who have helped me with this project. I am deeply grateful to Dr. Irawati Karvé, Chairman of the Department of Sociology and Anthropology at Deccan College Postgraduate and Research Institute, Poona, India. Dr. Karvé took time out of her busy schedule to give me valuable suggestions for this study. During this stay in Poona, Dr. Y. B. Damle, Dr. Samuel David, Dr. C. R. Sankaran, and Dr. Pramod Gadre were extremely helpful, especially in their critical analyses of the project. Dr. Vilas Adinath Sangave, Chairman of the Department of Sociology and Anthropology at Shivaji University at Kolhapur, read the manuscript and offered valuable criticism.

My colleagues and friends, in particular Floyd Martinson, Rodney Dannehl, Rufus T. Logan, C. F. Vikner, Alex Simirenko, Rajnikant Gandhi, Edward Rybnicek, Robert Zeller, Joel Torstenson, Russell Rosendahl, Lawrence Londer,

William Anderson, and Walter Ford, contributed much to this study.

Edith Tarcov, Sandra Sherwood, Janet Goldberg, Dolores Buelow, and Linda Turner helped with the manuscript preparation.

Frederick B. Tolles and Dorothy G. Harris of the Friends Historical Library of Swarthmore College provided me with valuable research material, as did the librarians of the Ames Library of Southeast Asia of the University of Minnesota.

Profound thanks are due to Dr. and Mrs. Don Martindale, without whom the study would not have been possible. Dr. Martindale's fellowship and writings have enriched my life. My thanks to him for writing the Foreword.

PART ONE

WEBER'S
THESIS

1

RELIGION AND ECONOMIC BEHAVIOR

Though the words "religion" [1] and "economics" suggest distinct provinces of thought and experience, it is said that "you cannot serve God and mammon." The basic interplay between religious and economic behavior has been established by some of the major sociologists of the twentieth century. Max Weber, one of the most prominent, studied the economic ethics of Hinduism, Taoism, Buddhism, Christianity, Judaism, and Islam to test hypotheses first formulated in *The Protestant Ethic and the Spirit of Capitalism,* his classic study of the relation between religion and the economic behavior in the West. [2]

Weber was interested in the combination of circumstances responsible for the cultural uniqueness of Western civilization. He thought this uniqueness was related to the process of rationalization in the West. He theorized that the religious ethic of the Puritan middle-class man was a major factor in the rise of modern industrial capitalism. To test his theories,

3

Weber undertook comparative studies of India and China where, in spite of many favorable factors, industrial capitalism failed to develop.[3] In the East, the process of rationalization was largely wanting, as were various other phenomena often associated with it. Indian geometry, for example, had no rational proofs. Moreover, the Indian sciences, though well developed in observation, lacked the method of experiment. Though highly developed in empirical technique, medicine lacked a biological and, particularly, a biochemical foundation. A rational chemistry has been absent from all areas of culture except the West. Rationalism, thus, was central to the complex.

When he compared the Indian political thought with that of Aristotle, Weber found it lacking a systematic method comparable to that of Aristotle. The Indian School of Mimamsa, along with the extensive codification of the Near East—including the Indian books of law—lacked rigorous systematic forms of thought. In the field of music, rational tone intervals have been known in many world areas but they never evolved into rational harmonious music, having both counterpoint and harmony: "Our orchestra, with its string quartet as a nucleus, and the organization of ensembles of wind instruments; our bass accompaniment; our system of notation . . . all these things are known only in the Occident." [4] Similarly, though the technical basis of architecture in the West was borrowed from the Orient, Weber pointed to the lack of solution of the problem of the dome and "that type of classic rationalization of all art—in painting by the rational utilization of lines and spatial perspective—which the Renaissance created for us." [5] He further observed that, although there was printing in China, literature designed only for print—such as the press and periodical literature—failed to appear in the East. Finally, although political and social groups have existed as organizations for exerting influence and gaining power in many parts of the world, Weber emphasized the fact that:

> The State itself, in the sense of a political association with a rational, written constitution, rationally ordained law, and an administration bound to rational rules or laws, administered by trained officials, is known, in this combination of characteristics, only in the Occident, despite all other approaches to it.[6]

For Weber, this process of rationalization was the most fateful force in contemporary economic life. Capitalism, which initially embodied this rational process, involves much more than the impulse to acquire that may be found even among beggars, prostitutes, public officials and gamblers. Capitalism consists of more than taking advantage of opportunities for profit-making.

> Capitalism is identical with the pursuit of profit, and foreever *renewed* profit, by means of continuous, rational, capitalistic enterprise. . . . The important fact is always that a calculation of capital in terms of money is made, whether by modern book-keeping methods or in any other way, however primitive and crude. Everything is done in terms of balances: at the beginning of the enterprise an initial balance, before every individual decision a calculation to ascertain its probable profitableness, and at the end a final balance to ascertain how much profit has been made.[7]

Capitalism rests on the inclination of men to adopt certain types of practical, rational conduct. Since the magical and religious notions, as well as the ethical ideas of duty based upon them, have influenced the conduct of all men in the past, Weber reasoned that religious ideas may also have influenced the development of the present Western economic system. Too, because rationalization played a central role in Western capitalism, Weber proposed to investigate the influence of religion on its development. He was led to explore "the connection of the spirit of modern economic life with the rational ethics of ascetic Protestantism." [8]

RELIGIOUS AFFILIATION AND
SOCIAL STRATIFICATION

When Weber examined religion and economics in Germany, he found that the business leaders, including technically and commercially trained personnel, were predominately Protestant. This predominance of Protestants in positions of ownership in German economic life could conceivably have been a product of inherited wealth. However, generally it appeared that Catholic parents of equivalent wealth did not provide their children with an equal amount of higher education. Furthermore, given the opportunity, Roman Catholics preferred to become master craftsmen, while Protestants preferred to work in the factories where they achieved positions requiring skill and administrative ability. Hence, Weber theorized that these differences were a product of the type of education and religious atmosphere present in the respective Catholic and Protestant communities.

The fact that Catholics did not participate as actively as Protestants in the business life of communities in which they were a minority was particularly striking. Normally, Weber observes, national and religious minorities seek to enter business life because they are excluded from political office or the service of the State:

> This has undoubtedly been true of the Poles in Russia and Eastern Prussia, who have without question been undergoing a more rapid economic advance than in Galicia. . . . It has . . . been true of the Huguenots in France under Louis XIV, the Nonconformists and Quakers in England, . . . the Jew for two thousand years. But the Catholics in Germany have shown no striking evidence of such a result of their position.[9]

Weber undertook investigating the "peculiarities . . . which might have resulted in the behaviour" described above.[10] He theorized that the ascetic characteristics illustrated most fully by the Calvinistic churches played an important part in the industrial and capitalistic development of Europe. Cecil Rhodes, for example, though brought up in a clergyman's family, showed that an ascetic upbringing did not hinder, but rather helped the capitalistic entrepreneur. The Spaniards, in fact, equated Calvinism with the promotion of trade. Sir William Petty, a seventeenth-century observer, regarded the Calvinistic diaspora as the seedbed of capitalistic economy. He speculated that the Calvinistic way of life was connected with the intensive development of business acumen. This Petty found to be true of other Protestant sects as well,

> whose otherworldliness is as proverbial as their wealth, especially the Quakers and the Mennonites. The part which the former have played in England and North America fell to the latter in Germany and the Netherlands. That in East Prussia Frederick William I tolerated the Mennonites as indispensable to industry, in spite of their absolute refusal to perform military service, is . . . most striking.[11]

This led Weber to assert that the relationship between the old Protestant spirit and the modern capitalistic culture is to be found in the special religious characteristics of Protestantism.

THE SPIRIT OF CAPITALISM

Weber wished to account not merely for a means of making one's way in the world, not even business astuteness, but the quality of an ethos, sustaining "the idea of a duty of the individual toward the increase of his capital, which is assumed as an end in itself." [12] Such an ethos not only encouraged commercial daring, but gave it the character of an ethical maxim. Weber was quite emphatic on the ethical aspect of the behavior of the early capitalistic entrepreneur who played so central a role in Western European and American capitalism. Although capitalism occasionally appeared in China, India, and Babylon in antiquity, and in the Middle Ages, it lacked the above mentioned ethos. When noting that Ben Franklin praised honesty, industry, and punctuality as virtues because they indirectly assure credit, Weber observed that though Franklin claimed to be a Deist, he had a Calvinistic father. Thus, inadvertently, Franklin's desire for earning money, "so long as it is done legally, is the result and the expression of virtue and proficiency in a calling." [13]

In the period of its rise, modern capitalism required a certain type of discipline. This peculiar form of behavior was not only suited to the peculiarities of occasional individuals, but also to those of groups of men. The "spirit of capitalism" that characterized this behavior has been present throughout the United States. However, unlike the New England states where it is strong, the South did not seem to develop the ethos to a great degree. Weber attributes this to the fact that the New England colonies were founded by preachers and seminary graduates in whom the Protestant ethic was strong.

Acquisitive impulses are certainly not adequate to explain the rise of capitalism. The Italians were as acquisitive as were the Chinese Mandarins and the old Roman aristocrats, but capitalism did not develop among any of them. Of the Italian laborers, Weber says:

> The lack of *coscienziosità* of the labourers of such countries, for instance Italy as compared with Germany, has been, and to a certain extent still is, one of the principal obstacles to their capitalistic development.[14]

History offers numerous examples of ruthless acquisition in which ethical norms have been totally set aside, at least with respect to those outside of one's group. During times of war and piracy, all ethical considerations have often been set aside. Such acquisition lacks the principal character of early capitalism.

The most important opponent of the spirit of capitalism is traditionalism—satisfaction with a level of income even though one could acquire more. The traditional individual works to earn a living only to the extent necessary to take care of his habitual needs. "A man does not 'by nature' wish to earn more and more money, but simply to live as he is accustomed to live and to earn as much as is necessary for that purpose." [15] It was not possible to develop modern-type capitalism simply by increasing the intensity of labor. The difficulties encountered by modern industrial capitalists in India under the British administration illustrate this. The factory was introduced into India by the British. However, despite the

possibility of earning more, the Indian factory laborer chose
to work less. The Indian laborer was not interested in improving his standard of living; he was interested in securing
longer holidays and decorating his wife with jewelry. Instead
of saving, as soon as he had enough money he returned to his
home town and stayed there as long as he could afford to.
"He is simply a mere casual laborer. Discipline in the European sense is an unknown idea to him. Hence, in spite of a
fourfold cheaper wage, competition with Europe is maintained easily only in the textile industry, as two and a half
times as many workers and far more supervisors are
required." [16]

It was long believed that people work only as long as they
remain poor. This in turn was an excuse for low wages. However, low wages are not necessarily equivalent to cheap labor;
they may represent a false economy if output is correspond-
ingly low. For high output "labour must, on the contrary, be
performed as if it were an absolute end in itself, a calling.
But such an attitude is by no means a product of nature." [17]

THE PROTESTANT ETHIC

Weber used the expression the "spirit of modern capitalism"
to describe the attitude that seeks profit rationally and systematically. Handicraft enterprise is a partial early example of
the spirit of capitalism.

The predominant bearers of this peculiar attitude were
originally found among the rising strata of the lower industrial middle classes rather than among the commercial aristocrats.[18] The classical representatives "were not the elegant
gentlemen of Liverpool and Hamburg, with their commercial
fortunes handed down for generations, but the self-made

parvenus of Manchester and Westphalia, who often rose from very modest circumstances." [19]

The transition of a typical business or profession conducted in a traditionalistic manner to a modern capitalistic venture may be illustrated by the textile industry. A young man enters the family business and goes into the country to recruit weavers. By greatly increasing the vigor of his supervision of their labor, he turns them from peasants into laborers. Simultaneously, he begins to change his marketing methods. He personally solicits customers periodically and gears his products to their needs. Low prices and a large turnover are simultaneously introduced. "There was repeated what everywhere and always is the result of such a process of rationalization: those who would not follow suit had to go out of business." [20] When such an enterprise created a respectable fortune, the money was not consumed or lent out at interest, but reinvested in the business. Often an individual borrowed capital from his relatives to set this process into motion. It is immaterial where one obtains the capital to start one's business. What matters is the development of the peculiar psychological complex of the spirit of capitalism. If this spirit exists, it tends to express itself in the form of capitalistic enterprise.

Along with clear vision (rationality), the ethical qualities were essential to win the confidence of customers and workers if capitalism was to arise. The ideal early capitalistic businessman avoided ostentation and unnecessary expenditures. He was embarrassed by the outward signs of social recognition given him. He was modest and "distinguished by a certain ascetic tendency. . . . He gets nothing out of his wealth for himself, except the irrational sense of having done his job well." [21]

The original requisite of a capitalistic system was an intense devotion to calling. Today, it is no longer necessary to call upon religious forces to sustain economic life, because he who does not follow suit simply cannot be successful.[22] Once institutionalized, the capitalistic system no longer requires the spirit of capitalism.

Capitalistic circles in Florence were merely tolerated by the church since capitalism was opposed to its traditional attitudes. For the same reason, considerable sums were donated by the rich to religious institutions as conscience money. Weber found the comparison of Florence with Pennsylvania instructive. In Florence of the fourteenth and fifteenth centuries, the investing of money in the money market by the great political powers was considered ethically unjustifiable. However, in the eighteenth century in Pennsylvania, banking was considered the essence of correct moral conduct. In fact, it was viewed as a duty lest, for lack of money, a barter system be adopted.

Weber states that the background for acceptance of activity, which is apparently directed toward profit alone as a calling, is best understood as an aspect of the development of rationalism as a whole. He further states: "Rationalism is an historical concept which covers a whole world of different things. It will be our task to find out whose intellectual child the particular concrete form of rational thought was, from which the idea of a calling and the devotion to labour in the calling has grown." [23] Weber laid major stress on the origin of the rational component in the conception of a calling.

THE PROTESTANT PRINCIPLES
OF THE REFORMATION

The Reformation destroyed the universal culture of Europe which was characterized by the use of Latin as a language. It also personalized the ethical component of religion. This personalization was carried through in the notion of justification by faith.

The justification of religious conduct on the basis of individual faith rather than through an institution, entailed a restatement of religious values. Both Luther and Calvin were interested in what Jesus said. Both leaders differed from the Roman Catholic theologians who conceived salvation as possible only through the Roman Catholic Church. The Protestants had a different solution: justification (salvation) by faith, which made it an affair only of the individual.

New concern with individual conscience flowed from Protestantism's doctrine of justification by individual faith. The starting point for salvation was the conscience and not the adherence to institutional requirements—paying dues and the performance of outward sacraments.

Justification by faith and concern with the individual conscience changed the meaning of "grace" (i.e., "religious worthiness"). According to Roman Catholic notions, to identify oneself with the Church is to realize the grace of God. The Protestants, by contrast, conceived of a covenant between God and each individual. There was no need to identify oneself with any set of laws or an institution. Grace is an unmediated relationship to God.

All these ideas were synthesized in the Protestant concept of "vocation." Positions in the world ceased religiously to have different values. All vocations are of equal value—not good, better or best. In God's economy, being a shoemaker is as significant as being a priest. Lutheranism denies that priesthood is fundamentally more important than other roles. The grace of God is distributed on the basis of personal worthiness alone. Thus, Protestantism involves a denial of the power of the priest to dispense grace. Luther's claim was made at a time when the priesthood had highest claims to prestige.

However, Weber maintains that Luther can hardly be credited with possessing the spirit of capitalism. Though one might trace the beginnings of the transformation to capitalism to the Reformation, religious circles have not been friendly toward capitalism. Ben Franklin's point of view, for example, could not have appealed to Luther: on more than one occasion Luther declared himself to be opposed to usury or interest in any form.

LUTHER'S CONCEPT OF CALLING

The Reformation affected various Protestant churches in different ways. The authority of the Bible, from which Luther derived his particular idea of calling, placed an emphasis on economic traditionalism. "Everyone should abide by his living and let the godless run after gain. That is the sense of all the statements which bear directly on worldly activities." [24] Christ, as well as Paul, held the traditionalistic economic ideas. In the Lord's Prayer one is exhorted to pray, "Give us this day our daily bread," and an element of radical repudiation of pursuit of gain is found in the teachings of Christ. Since, according to Paul, the believer is expected to look forward to the eschatological hopes, he is exhorted to remain in the worldly occupation in which the call of the Lord found him. "Luther read the Bible through the spectacles of his whole attitude; at the time and in the course of his development from about 1518 to 1530 this not only remained traditionalistic but became ever more so." [25] Since Luther believed that everyone is called to some occupation, he maintained that it is the person's duty to wait for this call and to serve God in this respect.

Weber grants that although this equalitarian approach to calling does not in any way minimize the Lutheran form of the renewal of the religious life, Luther's concept of the calling most certainly had some practical significance. "Only that significance evidently cannot be derived directly from the attitude of Luther and his Church to worldly activity, and is perhaps not altogether so easily grasped as the connection with other branches of Protestantism." [26]

One cannot fully understand the Reformation without considering Luther's own personality, religious development, and spiritual influence. However, Weber states most emphatically that without Calvinism, Luther's work could not have had a full effect on the economic life of contemporary man.

While Weber takes as his starting point the investigation of the relationship between the old Protestant ethic and the psychology of capitalism, the works of Calvin, and the other leaders of Puritan sects, he does not imply that the founders of these religious movements were directly interested in the promotion of the spirit of capitalism. Menno, George Fox, and Wesley, to name a few, were primarily concerned with the salvation of the soul. These men upheld ethical ideals based entirely on religious motives. Weber maintains that "the cultural consequences of the Reformation were to a great extent, . . . unforseen and even unwished-for results of the labours of the reformers." [27]

In treating the Reformation as an active component in Western development, Weber wished to free his readers from the idea that the Reformation was a necessary result of economic changes.[28]

> We have no intention whatever of maintaining such a
> foolish and doctrinaire thesis as that the spirit of capitalism
> (in the provisional sense of the term explained above)
> could only have arisen as the result of certain effects of
> the Reformation, or even that capitalism as an economic
> system is a creation of the Reformation. . . . The fact
> that certain important forms of capitalistic business organi-
> zation are known to be considerably older than the Ref-
> ormation is a sufficient refutation of such a claim. On the
> contrary, we only wish to ascertain whether and to what
> extent religious forces have taken part in the qualitative
> formation and the quantitative expansion of that spirit
> over the world. Furthermore, what concrete aspects of our
> capitalistic culture can be traced to them.[29]

THE PRACTICAL ETHICS OF THE
ASCETIC BRANCHES OF PROTESTANTISM

According to Weber, there have been four principle forms of
ascetic Protestantism: "(1) Calvinism in the form which it
assumed in the main area of its influence in Western Europe,
especially in the seventeenth century; (2) Pietism; (3) Methodism; (4) the sects growing out of the Baptist movement." [30]
All gave rise to "psychological sanctions which, originating
in religious belief and the practice of religion, gave a direction
to practical conduct and held the individual to it." [31]

The influence of the various branches of ascetic Protestantism on practical conduct can best be approached by way of
the doctrine of predestination, formulated most sharply by
the Calvinists. Great political and cultural struggles of the
sixteenth and seventeenth centuries were fought over Calvinism in England, the Netherlands, and France. The doctrine
of predestination was Calvinism's most characteristic dogma.
The Westminster Confession formulates the doctrine as
follows:

> God from all eternity did by the most wise and holy counsel of His own will, freely and unchangeably ordain whatsoever comes to pass; yet so thereby neither is God the author of sin, nor is violence offered to the will of the creatures, nor is the liberty or contingency of second causes taken away, but rather established. Although God knows whatsoever may or can come to pass upon all supposed conditions; yet hath He not decreed any thing because He foresaw it as future, or as that which would come to pass upon such conditions.[32]

This doctrine of predestination presents the purpose of God as absolute and unconditional, independent of the whole finite creation, and as originating solely in the eternal counsel of His will. God is conceived as a great and mighty king who has appointed the course of nature and who directs the course of history, down to its minutest detail. His decree is eternal, unchangeable, holy, wise, and sovereign. It extends not merely to the course of the physical work, but to every event in history from the creation to the last judgment, and includes all the activities of the saints and angels in heaven and of the reprobates and demons in hell. Everything outside of God Himself is included in this all-embracing decree. It provides a providential control under which all things are hastening to the end of God's determining. The goal is one divine event toward which the whole of creation moves.

Because all finite creation exists as a medium through which God manifests His glory, and because it is absolutely dependent on Him, it of itself could originate no conditions which would limit or defeat the manifestation of that glory. From all eternity, God has purposed to do exactly what He is doing. He is the sovereign ruler of the universe and "does according to His will in the army of heaven and among the inhabitants of the earth; and none can stay His hand or say unto Him, 'What doest thou?' " [33] Because the universe had its origin in God and depends on Him for its continued existence, it must always be subject to His control so that nothing can come to pass contrary to what He expressly decrees or permits. Thus, the eternal purpose is represented as an act of sovereign predestination or foreordination, unconditioned by any subsequent fact or change in time.

The Reformed theologians saw the hand of God in every event of history and in all the workings of physical nature. The world was the complete realization of the eternal ideal. The world, as a whole, was brought into a unity by the governing, all-pervading, all-harmonizing, divine glory. While they visualized a divine ordering of the whole course of history to the last detail, the Reformed theologians were especially concerned with its relation to man's salvation. Calvin, the most important theologian of the Reformation, put the matter thus:

> Predestination we call the eternal decree of God, by which He has determined in Himself, what He would have to become of every individual of mankind. For they are not all created with a similar destiny; but eternal life is foreordained for some and eternal death for others. Every man, therefore, being created for one or the other of these ends, we say he is predestined either to life or to death. [34]

The doctrine of predestination gave every aspect of life an intensified religious significance. No item of everyday conduct remained religiously neutral.

The Reformation was essentially a revival of Augustinianism and, through it, evangelical Christianity again came into its own. Luther, the first leader of the Reformation, was an Augustinian monk and it was from the theology of his order that he derived his great principle of justification by faith alone. Luther, Calvin, Zwingli, and all of the other outstanding reformers of the period were in basic agreement. In his work *The Bondage of the Will,* Luther stated the doctrine of predestination in as emphatic and extreme a form as can be found among any of the reformed theologians. In his earlier writings, Philipp Melanchthon (1497-1560), German scholar and religious reformer, designated predestination as the fundamental principle of Christianity. He later modified this position, however, and brought in a kind of synergism in which God and man were supposed to cooperate in the process of salvation. The position taken by the early Lutheran Church was gradually modified until Lutherans eventually dropped the doctrine altogether and denounced it in its Calvinistic form. They came to hold a doctrine of universal grace and universal atonement; this has since become the accepted doctrine of the Lutheran Church.

Calvin built on the foundation that Luther laid. Luther stressed salvation by faith, his fundamental principle being more or less subjective and anthropological. Calvin stressed the principle of the sovereignty of God, and developed a principle which was more objective and theological. Lutheranism was more the religion of man who had found salvation after a long and painful search and who was content simply to bask in the sunshine of God's presence. Calvinism, not content to stop there, pressed on to ask how and why God had saved man.

The teaching of the Westminster Confession throws light upon the efficacious grace in the following manner:

> All those whom God has predestinated unto life, and those only, He is pleased, in His appointed and accepted time,

> effectually to call, by His work and Spirit, out of that state
> of death, in which they are by nature, to grace and salva-
> tion by Jesus Christ; enlightening their minds . . . taking
> away their heart of stone, and giving them a heart of flesh;
> renewing their wills, and by His almighty power determin-
> ing them to that which is good.[35]

For Calvin, this effectual call is of God's free and special grace alone, and not from anything foreseen in man. Man is totally passive until he is quickened or made alive, renewed by the Holy Spirit; he is then in a position to answer the call and to embrace the grace offered by it. The Calvinists held that the condition of men since the fall is such that, if left to themselves, they would continue in their state of rebellion and refuse all offers of salvation: Christ would then have died in vain. The Holy Spirit operates on the chosen to bring them to repentance and faith, and make them heirs of eternal life.

The lot of those not chosen was described by Calvin as follows:

> As for those wicked and ungodly men, whom God as a
> righteous judge, for former sins doth blind and harden,
> from them He not only with-holdeth His grace whereby
> they might have enlightened in their understandings and
> wrought upon in their hearts, but sometimes also with-
> draweth the gifts which they had and exposeth them to
> such objects as their corruption makes occasion of sin:
> and withal, gives them over to their own lusts, the tempta-
> tions of the world, and the power of Satan: whereby it
> comes to pass that they harden themselves, even under
> those means, which God useth for the softening of others.[36]

John Milton, for one, held a low opinion of this doctrine: "Though I may be sent to Hell for it, such a God will never command my respect." [37]

SYSTEMS OPPOSED TO CALVINISM

It would be profitable at this stage in the discussion to examine briefly two systems opposed to Calvinism—namely, Universalism and Arminianism.

Universalism is the view that Christ died for all men, and that eventually all will be saved, either in this life or through a future probation. This view perhaps makes the strongest appeal to one's emotions. Probably only certain sects have held this view, and it appears that Protestant denominations have usually rejected it.

Arminianism held that Christ died equally and indiscriminately for every human individual—for those who perish no less than for those who are saved. Election is not an eternal and unconditional act of God but rather a saving grace that is offered to every man, to receive or reject as he pleases. Man may successfully resist the regenerating power of the Holy Spirit if he chooses, for the saving grace is not necessarily permanent. Those who are loved of God, ransomed by Christ, and born again of the Holy Spirit may still throw away all and perish eternally.

In its radical form, Arminianism is a recrudescence of Pelagianism, a type of self-salvation. Some scholars believe that Arminianism can be traced back to Pelagianism as definitively as Calvinism to Augustinianism since the principles of Pelagianism were brought into existence 1,200 years before Arminius was born. Pelagianism denied human depravity, the necessity of efficacious grace, and exalted the human will above the divine.

Arminianism attempted a compromise between the systems of Pelagius and Augustine. Its main idea was that man is weak because of the Fall, but it denied that all capacity for salvation has been lost. Man, therefore, merely needs divine grace to assist his personal efforts. Man is feeble but not dead. Unaided, he indeed cannot help himself but he can engage the help of a physician and can either accept or reject the help when it is offered. Man is in a position to cooperate with the grace of God in the matter of salvation. This view exalts man's freedom at the expense of God's sovereignty. While Arminianism admires the dignity and strength of man, Calvinism is most concerned with the grace and omnipotence of God.

In Calvinism, men exist for God and not God for the sake of men. "All creation, including of course the fact, as it undoubtedly was for Calvin, that only a small proportion of men are chosen for eternal grace, can have any meaning only as means to the glory and majesty of God." [38] The Arminians hold that Christ died for all men alike, while the Calvinists believe that in the secret plan of God, Christ died for the elect only, and that His death had only an incidental reference to others in so far as they are partakers of common grace. The Westminster Confession states:

> Wherefore they who are elected being fallen in Adam, are redeemed in Christ, are effectually called unto faith in Christ by His Spirit working in due season; are justified, adopted, sanctified, and kept by His power through faith unto salvation. Neither are any other redeemed by Christ, effectually called, justified, adopted, sanctified, and saved but the elect only.[39]

Calvinists argue that this doctrine necessarily follows from the doctrine of election. God has predetermined not to save some as truly as, and in the same sense as, Christ was sent to die for those whom He had chosen for salvation. If God has elected some and not others to eternal life, then plainly the primary purpose of Christ's work was to redeem the elect.

> For the damned to complain of their lot would be much the same as for animals to bemoan the fact they were not born as men. . . . God's grace is, since His decrees cannot change, as impossible for those to whom He has granted it to lose as it is unattainable for those to whom He has denied it.[40]

The effect of this doctrine upon the individual during the Reformation was to intensify concern with the question of one's own eternal salvation. Predestination meant that man's fate was already decided. Indeed, Weber echoes the thought which must have passed through the mind of the man of this period: "There was no one to help him." Unlike the Catholic who could take comfort in the priest and the church, the individual stood alone. One could not turn to God and expect mercy, for the decree had already been made regarding one's election; Christ had died only for the elect. Klotsche and Mueller, Church historians, observe that "Calvin's theory of the certainty of salvation either makes men self-confident and secure or drives them to despair." [41] The Puritan could not satisfactorily resort to any magical means to attain salvation or indulge in any superstition whatsoever. Sacraments were no comfort to him. The old Hebrew prophets initiated the process of elimination of magic from the world. The Protestants, with the aid of Hellenistic scientific thought, consummated the process by repudiating all magical means to salvation as superstitions. Weber remarks that "there was not only no magical means of attaining the grace of God for those to whom God had decided to deny it, but no means whatever." [42]

A peculiar, deeply spiritual isolation was pronounced by

the Protestant ethic. Bunyan's *Pilgrim's Progress* is an excellent description of the Puritan life. The faithful Puritan is seen as being first and foremost concerned with his own salvation. Only after he secures it, and has the assurance that his salvation is secure, does he think of his family. He is not his brother's keeper—that is an affair of his brother's conscience.

Calvinism provides for social organization as a by-product of its principles. The individual is concerned, as depicted in Bunyan's *Pilgrim's Progress,* with his own salvation. However, in providing for his own "calling and election," [43] he cannot think only of himself. Benjamin Warfield, a theologian of the Reformed Church, says:

> We can never know that we are elected of God to eternal life except by manifesting in our lives the fruits of election—faith and virtue, knowledge and temperance, patience and godliness, love of the brethren. . . . It is idle to seek assurance of election outside of holiness of life.[44]

Good works assured the Calvinist of his faith and increased his certainty of salvation. It has been said that, while Luther and Calvin are in general agreement concerning the relation of good works to justification, there are differences in their conception of the source, the standard, and the purpose of good works.[45] For Calvin, faith is not the propelling cause of the elect's life. He attributes man's sanctification to the influence of the Holy Spirit. Luther, however, lays the emphasis on justifying faith as the spontaneous source of actions that are pleasing to the Lord.

Both Luther and Calvin agree that the law of God is the rule of life and conduct; however, they differ in their emphasis. Luther believed that it is the love of Christ that constrains men to do good toward everyone. Words such as "commandment," "law," "duty," "servant," and "obedience" frequently occur in Calvin's writings, indicating his view that the Christian acts not out of love but out of fear. Moreover, Luther does not emphasize the glorification of God as the object and end of good works. For Calvin, the activity of the Christian in the world is explained solely in the glorification of God. One is not chosen because he is good, but rather in order that he might become good. Good works are His glory.

Predestination for Calvin applies to the physical world. Weber remarks:

> For the wonderfully purposeful organization and arrange-
> ment of this cosmos is, according both to the revelation of
> the Bible and to natural intuition, evidently designed by
> God to serve the utility of the human race. This makes
> labour in the service of impersonal social usefulness appear
> to promote the glory of God and hence to be willed by
> Him.[46]

Weber suggests that the decisive problem is: "How was this doctrine borne in an age to which the after-life was not only more important, but in many ways also more certain, than all the interests of life in this world?" [47] Every believer was expected to ask himself, "Am I one of the elect?" All other questions were secondary. For Calvin, this may not have been a problem; it appears from his writings that he was quite confident of his own election to eternal life. Calvin never suggested that the believers possessed any special subjective experience superior to that of nonbelievers. Outwardly they were no different from nonbelievers.

Calvin regarded the church as the totality of the elect of all ages and places. The church was invisible and an object of faith. The believers are found in an empirical communion—the visible church—consisting of all those who profess to be believers. The visible church is to be respected; withdrawal from the visible church is, therefore, also a denial of God and Christ.

It was natural that the average person would desire to be one of the elect. Men and women sought an infallible criteria of membership in the elect; certainty in this respect was helpful for administering the Lord's Supper. According to Calvin, a sacrament is more than a mere ritual; it is an outward sign by which God signifies the promises of His grace, and men, in turn, express their devotion toward Him. It is the elect alone who receive spiritually, through faith, the body and blood in the Lord's Supper; the unbelievers receive mere bread and wine. According to Calvin, "this sacred bread of the Lord's Supper is to be spiritual food to the sincere worshippers of God [and] . . . is changed into a most obnoxious poison to all whose faith it does not nourish." [48] Similarly, baptism is necessary because it is commanded by Christ. However, baptism in itself does not save any one, not even children. Baptism is only an added seal, not to provide efficacy to the promise of God as if it possessed validity in itself, but only to confirm it to mankind.

The followers did not have to be satisfied with Calvin's trust in the testimony of the expectant faith that resulted from grace. His pastoral advice to the members of the congregation was:

> On the one hand it is held to be an absolute duty to consider oneself chosen, and to combat all doubts as temptations of the devil, since lack of self-confidence is the result of insufficient faith, hence of imperfect grace. . . . On

the other hand, in order to attain that self-confidence intense worldly activity is recommended as the most suitable
means. . . . It alone disperses religious doubts and gives
the certainty of grace.[49]

The worldly activities of the individual are not only considered capable of giving certainty of grace but are also
positively encouraged and expected. The individual is expected not only to pray but also to undertake good works, as
exhorted by Paul: "Finally, brethren, whatsoever things are
true . . . whatsoever things are just . . . whatsoever things
are of good report; if there be any virtue, and if there be any
praise, think on these things." "With quietness they
work . . . not weary in well doing." [50] The doctrine of
predestination did not make men indolent and careless, but
energized and stimulated them to redoubled efforts. On the
practical results of the doctrine of predestination, J. B.
Mozley, nineteenth-century Presbyterian theologian, says:

> The person as soon as he regards himself as predestined to
> achieve some great object, acts with much greater force and
> constancy for the attainment of it; he is not divided by
> doubts, or weakened by scruples or fears; he believes fully
> that he shall succeed, and that belief is the greatest assistance
> to success. It must be observed that this is true of the moral
> and spiritual, as well as of the natural man, and applied
> to religious aims and purposes as well as to those connected
> with human glory.[51]

Earl Haig, Commander-in-Chief of the British armies in
the First World War, who was a Scotsman and a Calvinistic
Presbyterian, regarded himself, in true Calvinistic fashion, as
the predestinated instrument of divine providence for the
achievement of victory for the British armies. His native self-

reliance was reinforced by his concept of himself as the child of destiny.

A Calvinist does not believe that good works in themselves secure salvation. Paul said, "work out your own salvation with fear and trembling, for it is God which worketh in you both to will and to do of His good pleasure." [52] This was interpreted to mean that after having achieved salvation by faith and God's election, one gives evidence of it in his own life. Nonetheless salvation could be secured by election alone. Works are but evidence of the salvation already obtained. Good works rid one of the fear of damnation, thus allowing man to enjoy real peace with his Maker. To the Calvinist, good works have a psychological rather than soteriological value.

The Catholic ethic is one of intentions in which each single good or bad action is credited with helping determine a man's temporal and eternal fate. To the Catholic, the church existed in order to help him in each crisis. The sacraments were no mere symbols, but actually bestowed grace upon the individual. Individual good acts could receive indulgences. For the Calvinist, the means of grace was not supplied through the agency of the church. For practical purposes, he was alone with his Maker. Hence, the Calvinist was not satisfied with individual good acts, but was concerned rather with a life of good works combined into a unified system. Every moment of every day was to be lived for the glory of God. Weber says: "The life of the saint was directed solely toward a transcendental end, salvation. But precisely for that reason it was thoroughly rationalized in this world and dominated entirely by the aim to add to the glory of God on earth." [53]

This sort of religiously rationalized life was characteristic of Western monasticism. The monks of the Middle Ages were unlike those of the East. In the Orient, monasticism was planless, otherworldly, and irrational, permeated by self-torture. The monk in the West was trained objectively as a worker in the service of God. This assured the monk of the salvation of his soul. The Puritan who practiced a rational type of asceticism proved by his life that it was entirely possible to be ascetic and yet lead an alert and intelligent life.

In contrast to medieval monasticism, modern Calvinism was founded on an ascetic life that was not limited to the monk alone. The individual—any individual who cared enough for his salvation—could pursue an ascetic life. Sebastian Frank remarked that the Reformation made every Christian a monk for the rest of his life. The monks stressed spiritual supremacy; the Calvinists added something new—namely, "the idea of the necessity of proving one's faith in worldly activity." [54] Henceforth, not only the spiritual activity of the monk was counted worthy of emulation, but also the spiritual aristocracy of the predestined saints of God, not withdrawn from, but within the world.

The Old and the New Testaments are regarded by Calvin as being equally important. It is not "left to faithful ministers to frame any new doctrine . . . but simply to adhere to the doctrine to which God has made all subject." The rational suppression of the mystical and the emotional side of religion has been attributed by Sanford to the influence of the Old Testament.[55]

The Reformed Christian was constantly occupied with the progress of his own spiritual life. He observed the Hand of the Lord in all things. "All things work together for good to those that love God . . ." "Servants, obey in all things your

masters, not with eye service, as men pleasers; but in single-
ness of heart, fearing God: And whatsoever ye do, do it
heartily, as to the Lord, and not unto men." [56] Having a
godly servant was a very wise policy on the part of the employer because the interests of the employer were identical
with those of the Lord. Thus, there was no need for
supervision.

The desire to glorify God not only affected employer-
employee relationships, but also influenced those between
husband and wife, children and parents. "Husbands love
your wives . . . Wives submit to your husbands. . . . Children obey your parents in all things; for this is well pleasing
unto the Lord." [57] This constant examination of one's own
conduct "could thus almost take on the character of a business
enterprise." [58] The Puritan methodically rationalized his entire life. The doctrine of predestination, thus, assumed practical significance by forming a psychological basis for rational
morality.

The moral standards of some of the Lutheran princes were
deplorable. Unlike their Reformed counterparts, some de-
graded themselves with drunkenness and vulgarity, and were
abetted by the Lutheran clergy who put far too much emphasis
on faith alone. Calvinism, by contrast, instilled a very definite
ascetic tendency in a person's life. According to Weber,
Lutheranism's doctrine of grace lacked the full psychological
sanction of systematic conduct compelling the methodical
rationalization of life. Weber admits freely that the Calvinistic
doctrine was only one of several possibilities contained in
Protestantism, but in it Protestantism's peculiar psychological
effects were extraordinarily powerful. "In comparison with it
the non-Calvinistic ascetic movements, considered purely

from the view-point of the religious motivation of asceticism, form an attenuation of the inner consistency and power of Calvinism." [59]

Pietism

Around the middle of the seventeenth century, Roman Catholics as well as Protestants became dissatisfied with formal doctrine and the manner of life of professing Christians. Movements developed which stressed piety and a rededicated way of life. In France, there was a revival of Augustinianism in opposition to Jesuitism and the worldly tendencies of the church. The name "Pietists" was initially used as a nickname. Its devotees were ridiculed as were the early Christian disciples.

Philip Spener (1635-1705) was the leader of the Pietistic movement in the Lutheran Church. Long before Spener, sects in England and Holland had arisen that were opposed to emphasizing dogma as a substitute for holiness and discipline. Gisbert Voet, a leading Dutch theologian of this period, spoke of the "puritanism" exercised in the conventicles of the regenerate as "the exact and perfect agreement of human actions with the law prescribed by God, accepted by real believers and followed with zeal." [60] Devotional literature was found in great abundance at this time, such as John Bunyan's *Pilgrim's Progress,* John Arndt's *True Christianity,* Richard Baxter's *Saint's Everlasting Rest,* and Louis Bayly's *Practice of Piety.*

Although justification by faith was a central doctrine of the Lutheran Church, Spener felt that religion was not a matter of knowledge, but of practice. The Pietists, on the whole, blurred the distinction between justification and sanctification. They felt that only a living faith, evidenced in a pious life, could attain justification. Klotsche and Mueller assert that "in their striving after sanctification, they lost sight of the meaning of justification." [61] The Pietists were of the opinion that in order to teach theology, one must first become a model of piety. Thus, the mere learning and formal acceptance of creeds was made secondary to leading a pious life.

The influence of Pietism was felt up to the middle of the eighteenth century. Nicholas von Ludwig Zinzendorf (1700–1760), Spener's godson and a former Lutheran minister, was ordained a bishop of the Moravian Church which became a bastion of pietism. "This is in keeping with their tendency to make Christianity pre-eminently a matter of feeling." [62]

Compared with Calvinism, the rationalization of life by Pietism was necessarily less intense because of the preoccupation with a state of grace. Concern with the future and with eternity intensified emotional emphasis. The assurance of his election motivated the true Calvinist to strive to be successful at his calling. The Pietist, on the other hand, lacked the incentive to achieve economic success due to his attitude of humility and abnegation.

The virtues of Pietism, according to Weber, may be regarded as those cherished by the faithful official, clerk, laborer or domestic worker. Calvinism, on the other hand, was more closely related to the active enterprise of bourgeois, capitalistic entrepreneurs.

Methodism

John and Charles Wesley were the founders of the Methodist movement. In 1729 while reading the Bible, these two young

Englishmen concluded that they could not be saved without holiness; thus, they "followed after it, and incited others to do so. In 1737 they saw, likewise, that men are justified before they are sanctified; but still holiness was their object. God then thrust them out to raise a holy people." [63] (This is their own description.) Before the end of the century, they came to be known as "evangelicals" and those who left the established church in England were known as the "Methodists."

The distinguishing characteristic of Methodism is the emphasis on an emotional though ascetic type of religion with a tendency to free itself from the dogmatic character of Calvinism. In order to receive an assurance of salvation, methodical conduct was considered most desirable. On his visit to America, John Wesley was greatly impressed by the Moravian Pietists. He encountered them for the first time and observed the seriousness of their behavior, their patience, humility, and complete freedom from fear. Most of all, the Moravians maintained that faith is far from an intellectual assent to the truths of the Gospel, and far from a rational belief in the Christian way of life. Faith has nothing to do with the human act; it is the gift of God. Wesley's experience at Aldersgate and the influence of Moravian Pietism made him a new man. William R. Cannon, the biographer of John Wesley, remarked:

> The center of his religion had shifted from an interest in self and an evaluation of all life in terms of his own self-aggrandizement to a love of God . . . with this came an entirely new conception of justification. He no longer thought of it as the hard struggle of man to achieve by means of good works his own salvation with fear and trembling and thus to merit the gift of Christ's atonement; rather the free gift of faith bestowed on man.[64]

Wesley violently attacked predestination, affirming that this Calvinistic doctrine made all preaching vain. Preaching is of no value to the elected, for with or without it, they will be saved. On the other hand, it is meaningless to preach to those who are not elected for they are thought to be incapable of either grasping or perceiving the meaning of the Word. In fact, the doctrine of predestination could not be considered a doctrine of God since it destroys holiness, which, for Wesley, is the end of all the ordinances of God.

Calvinism regarded everything emotional with suspicion. Methodism, on the other hand, gave importance to the pure feeling of the absolute certainty of forgiveness. This subjective certainty was viewed as a witness of the Spirit, which in most cases could even be pinpointed to the hour. Weber is quick to point out that in spite of the great significance of self-evident feeling, righteous conduct according to the law was stressed. In 1771, Wesley declared that he who does not perform good works is not a true believer. He would often quote I John 3:9, which reads: "Whatsoever is born of God doth not commit sin; for His seed remaineth in him; and he cannot sin, because he is born of God." Moreover, the doctrine of sanctification came to be viewed as the "second blessing." A second deep spiritual experience, capable of further working of the divine grace in this life, gave a strong assurance of salvation; such an experience instilled confidence in the individual, helping him to overcome the typical Calvinistic anxiety.

The weak often assumed a fatalistic interpretation of Christian freedom: the self-confident often became very emotional. Wesley was influenced by the Lutherans via the Moravians, which increased the ambiguity of the religious basis of Methodist ethics. Methodism never placed much importance on the external means of grace; the sacraments, therefore, did not acquire a prominent place in the church. Conversion, too, was an emotional act. However, the Methodists were not encouraged to sit back and relax in quiet enjoyment of the emotional experience as professed by the Moravian Church. By arousing emotion through the experience of a second blessing, the Methodist was directed toward what Weber described as, "a rational struggle for perfection." Therefore, although emotional in character, the Methodist faith did not lead individuals to a religion as entirely spiritualized as that of Pietism.

According to Weber, the regeneration of Methodism involved only a supplement to the pure doctrine of works and provided a religious basis for ascetic conduct. Despite the rejection of the doctrine of predestination, Wesley agreed that the outward signs or the fruits of conversion were similar to those found among the adherents of Calvinism. For this reason, and also because of its recent origin as compared to Calvinism, Weber felt that Methodism did not basically change the idea of calling.

The Baptist Sects

If one takes Calvinism as a primary reference point, the Pietism of Continental Europe and the Methodism in England and America appear as secondary movements. However, the ascetic movement that arose independently within the Protestant churches, known as the Baptist movement, was hardly secondary. Offshoots of the movement include the Anabaptists, Mennonites, and Quakers.

The most important feature of Baptist doctrine is the

believer's church. The visible church, as in the time of the Reformation, was not considered important. As an institution, the church was not important even from the point of view of affirming the glory of God as the Calvinists would prefer to do. The church was not a medium of salvation to men, as the Lutherans and the Roman Catholics believed. It consisted solely of individuals who have personal faith in Christ and, thus, have been reborn. Weber, therefore, calls the Baptist churches "sects" rather than "churches." No Baptist is happy with this appellation. The Baptists quote St. Paul: "That He might present it to Himself a glorious church, not having any spot or wrinkle." [65] In this sense they form *the* church.

Weber regards them as sects because they lack all relation to the State. A religious community of this nature rests on the conviction that only those who were born of the Spirit of God could form part of the church. Since they believed in the complete separation of state and church, the Baptists' church could only be a voluntary organization. A church may be regarded as a natural social group similar to the family or the nation, while a sect is a voluntary association. A person is born into a church; an individual can only join a sect. In a very real sense, no one could be a Baptist or a member of any of the allied groups unless he made a personal decision to do so. Children born to Baptist parents are, as a rule, "dedicated" in the church, but are not baptized until adulthood when they have experienced the personal assurance of regeneration.

A desire to go back to the early Christian pattern of living meant, in reality, an avoidance of the world—that is, any unnecessary intercourse with worldly people. Moreover, all idolatry of the flesh was rejected by the Baptists. The Amish movement within the Mennonites is the most conservative wing of the Anabaptists. In Pennsylvania, they speak German, retain the culture of the seventeenth-century Swiss-Germans, and are opposed to modern conveniences such as automobiles, telephones, and modern educational institutions.

By following the pattern for his daily life as laid down in Scriptures, the individual was attuned to the Spirit of God that guided him in all walks of life. There was, thus, a continual illumination of the Word by the Holy Spirit. The Quakers developed the doctrine of the inner testimony of the Holy Spirit in reason and conscience. Weber asserts that this replaced their dependence upon the Bible as the ultimate authority, and initiated a development that radically modified the doctrine of salvation through the church. The Quakers have even gone so far as to do away with baptism and communion.

By a radical devaluation of the importance of the sacraments as a means to salvation, Weber points out that the Baptists "thus accomplished the religious rationalization of the world in its most extreme form." [66] Continual revelation was considered essential to understand the Scriptures. The verse often was I Corinthians 2:14: "The natural man receiveth not the things of the Spirit of God: for they are foolishness unto him: neither can he know them, because they are spiritually discerned." Natural reason, therefore, was of no avail; the individual remained a man of the flesh, and both Baptists and Quakers condemned this godlessness.

The influence of the Calvinistic asceticism was felt by the Baptist sects in England and the Netherlands. The Baptists stressed the importance of being pure, godly, and blameless before man and God. Although the gift of God could not be earned, one had to be true to the dictates of his own conscience. This, in turn, assured good works and was, thus, similar to the Calvinistic asceticism in its practical result.

The rational character of Calvinism was due to the influence of the doctrine of predestination. The Baptist communities had rejected predestination and yet produced a rational character. This type of morality, Weber says, "rested psychologically above all on the idea of expectant waiting for the Spirit to descend, which . . . is characteristic of the Quaker meeting." [67] Silent waiting has the most desirable effect on the individual. It helps a person overcome impulsiveness and irrationality and even subdue his passions. It also has certain side effects. The waiting period gives rise to the prophesying of members and their hoping for all sorts of unexpected things to take place in the future. For the purposes of this discussion, the most important result of inner meditation is that the individual tends to weigh different courses of action, and becomes concerned with being true to his conscience. Living in a period where one could not resort to magic to achieve salvation, the Baptist communities could only follow a form of worldly asceticism.

In its early days, worldliness was radically rejected. Eventually, as Weber mentions, the well-to-do bourgeois came to defend the practical worldly virtues and the system of private property. Weber points out that the strict morality of the Baptists had turned, in practice, to the path prepared by the Calvinistic ethic. Monastic forms of asceticism had come to be regarded as unscriptural, and had acquired the connotation of obtaining salvation by means of doing good works. This had to be avoided since this path had been rejected by Luther, who, in this respect, the Baptist communities felt was correct.

Certain Baptist sects—such as the Brethren (Dunkers)—traditionally refused to go to war, dressed in plainest clothing, insisted that their women cover their heads, and refrained from all worldly amusements. This, Weber concludes, had a dual effect. On the one hand, it weakened the Calvinistic concept of the calling as is the case with the Pietists. On the other hand, interest in economic occupations was augmented since they deliberately refused to go to war or take up work for their government. The only work open for these people was nonpolitical.[68] Plain living and high thinking, the motto of the Baptists, resulted in an antagonism towards any aristocratic way of life.

Weber draws attention to the immense importance of the Baptist doctrine of salvation. This doctrine stressed the role of conscience as the revelation of God to the individual, giving one's worldly conduct the character of a calling. This was of great significance to the development of the spirit of capitalism. The specific form of worldly asceticism of the Baptists—and in particular that of the Quakers—was expressed in the maxim, "Honesty is the best policy." The influence of Calvinism was exerted as a result of this, more in the liberation of energy than in private acquisition. The task now remains to trace the results of the Puritan idea of calling as it relates to the business world.

The mercantilistic regulations of the State might have developed industries, but without some outside help, these rules simply could not have developed the spirit of capitalism. Or, possibly, an ecclesiastical body may become so despotic that it may succeed in obtaining external conformity; simultaneously, however, it may weaken the subjective motives of rational conduct. The fact that the Baptist movement founded sects rather than churches only intensified their asceticism. H. Richard Niebuhr remarks:

> Furthermore, wealth frequently increases when the sect subjects itself to the discipline of asceticism in work and expenditure; with the increase of wealth the possibilities for culture also become more numerous and involvement in the economic life of the nation as a whole can less easily be limited.[69]

Weber concluded *The Protestant Ethic* by considering the effect of the religious ideas of ascetic Protestantism upon the rules laid down for everyday conduct. Life was given a systematic religious interpretation. Even a man's social position depended upon his relation to the religious community. It is almost impossible today to appreciate the way religious themes influenced the people at large. Weber said: "In such a time the religious forces which express themselves through such channels are the decisive influences in the formation of national character." [70]

For the sake of simplicity, Weber treats ascetic Protestantism as a whole. English Puritanism, which derived from Calvinism, can be used to illustrate the idea of calling. The universally known writer on the subject of the Puritan ethic, Richard Baxter (1615–1691), illustrates its practical impacts. Preoccupied with the problem of practical moral conduct, Baxter even offered his services to Cromwell's government.

Baxter's writings offer contrasts to Spener's *Theologische Bedenken,* since Spener represented German Pietism. In Baxter's books, *Saints' Everlasting Rest* and the *Christian*

Directory, he speaks of wealth as a great danger and its pursuit as senseless as compared with seeking the Kingdom of God. Furthermore, wealth is morally suspect. Asceticism is usually associated with a condemnation of the pursuit of money and goods. Calvin, in comparison, saw no harm in the acquisition of wealth; even for the clergy it was desirable and a source of prestige.

The Puritan objection to the pursuit of wealth was based on the theory that since the believer's destiny is in the world to come, while he is here on this earth he should work hard in order to be certain of his state of grace. Activity, not frivolous enjoyment, serves to increase the glory of God.

Time was precious and not to be wasted. Since life was very short, one had to work hard to insure one's salvation. Idle words were to be kept to the minimum. "Every idle word that men shall speak, they shall give an account thereof." [71] Quakers have often insisted that their children learn a calling because of the commandment, "With quietness they work and eat their own bread . . . if any would not work, neither should he eat." [72]

Baxter constantly recommended people to work hard in the approved ascetic technique. This has always been true to the Western church, in sharp contrast not only to the Orient but also to most monastic orders the world over. Even within marriage sexual intercourse was permitted only for the increase of the glory of God, since the commandment was: "Be fruitful, and multiply; and replenish the earth." [73] The effect of constant exhortation on Baxter's part was that labor was increasingly turned into an end in itself. Every man had to work; he who did not betrayed signs of lacking grace.

For Thomas Aquinas, labor had been only a means to an end. Every man did not necessarily have to work. Aside from accomplishing the necessary maintenance of the individual and the community, work had no special significance. Contemplation was a superior state to mere work.

For the Lutheran, work was a fate to which an individual had to submit. For the Puritan, on the other hand, whether he was rich or poor, God in His providence had prepared a calling. Also, the division of men into classes and occupations was accepted as an assignment from God. However, for the Puritans the providential purpose of the division of labor was to be known by its fruits.

Baxter, with definite Puritan character, commends the specialized worker because, unlike an unskilled laborer, he has a definite calling, is very methodical, is not idle, and has a clear goal before him. The Quaker view also stresses exercise in ascetic virtue. Through conscientiousness, a man's calling becomes a confirmation of the state of grace. "What God demands is not labour in itself, but rational labour in a calling." [74] The Puritan emphasizes methodical behavior; the Lutheran resigns himself to his lot as the will of God.

A man's calling is a stewardship bestowed by God. The faithful Christian at all times makes use of all opportunities. By success in his calling, he assures himself of the grace of God. A man must work hard; he must improve his talents and expect more in return for the use of his talents. "For unto every one that hath shall be given, and he shall have abundance: but from him that hath not shall be taken away even that which he hath." [75] As long as an individual did not misuse his wealth, he was expected to increase it as a proof of his state of grace.

The emphasis on the ascetic importance of a fixed calling provided an ethical justification for the modern specialized division of labor. The Puritan businessman also felt quite justified in augmenting his profits as he believed that the Lord rewarded his faithful servants. "Thy barns shall be filled with plenty, and thy presses shall burst out with new wine." "The Lord blessed Job . . . he had fourteen thousand sheep, and six thousand camels, and a thousand yoke of oxen, and a thousand she asses." [76] In whatever the good man did, he prospered. The Calvinist looked for God's blessing here and now—as did Job—and not merely for spiritual blessing.

The Old Testament was interpreted in terms of this idea of the calling. Elements within the Mosaic Law which the Puritans found difficult to reconcile with modern life were considered the exclusive domain of the Jewish people. The blessings of the Old Testament such as those mentioned in the Book of Deuteronomy, "Blessed shall be thy basket and thy store, the Lord shall open unto thee His good treasure, and bless all the work of thy hand," [77] were considered rewards of the ascetic life and valid for the modern man.

> The Jews stood on the side of the politically and speculatively oriented adventurous capitalism; their ethos was, in a word, that of pariah-capitalism. But Puritanism carried the ethos of the rational organization of capital and labour. It took over from the Jewish ethic only what was adapted to this purpose.[78]

The Puritans permitted nothing to interfere with their ascetic conduct. Sports were permitted only when they served a rational purpose—to improve the individual physically. All impulsive enjoyment was to be avoided if it hindered one's calling or if it was detrimental to rational asceticism. Dance halls and similar places were placed in this category.

Renaissance culture was emulated and given prominence in the discourses of the ministers. Higher education was considered desirable. The theatre and worldly arts represented idolatry of the flesh and therefore never received any encouragement at the hands of the Puritans. The "powerful tendency toward uniformity of life, which to-day so immensely aids the capitalistic interest in the standardization of production, had its ideal foundations in the repudiation of all idolatry of the flesh." [79]

While the individual was permitted to enjoy intellectual pleasures or indulge only in sports that had athletic value, the ministers warned the Puritan to beware of the stewardship of his talents and wealth. Wealth must not be squandered. No money must be spent on anything which does not glorify God. Denial of the temptations of the flesh, according to Barklay, was not a struggle against the rational acquisition, but only against the irrational use of the wealth the individual possessed.

If individuals could not squander their wealth, the inevitable result was the accumulation of capital, which was then made available for productive investment. Asceticism frowned upon wealth as an end in itself; however, simultaneously, it encouraged the attainment of wealth as a fruit of labor in a calling because this was a proof of God's blessing. The Puritan worked continuously and systematically in his calling; he regarded this as the way to asceticism and evidence of new birth.

Since the Puritan limited his consumption and, simultaneously, continued to accumulate wealth, the practical result was, as Weber puts it, "accumulation of capital through ascetic compulsion to save." [80] The very restraints upon the use of wealth resulted in its increase and this wealth made possible the productive investment of capital.

The feudal way of life held in high esteem the investment of wealth in land. This practice did not appeal to the Puritans, for although they had great respect for agriculture, this respect was reserved not for the landlord, but for the farmer, particularly for the rational individual cultivator. Against the glitter and ostentation of feudal magnificence, which rested on an unsound economic basis, the Puritan preferred a sober simplicity. There developed a manner of living consistent with the ideal of the middle-class home.

The whole history of monasticism is, in a certain sense, the history of a continual struggle with the problem of the secularizing influence of wealth. This is also true, on a larger scale, of the worldly asceticism of Puritans. Weber quotes John Wesley to support this theory. When riches increased, Wesley noticed that the spirit of religion normally decreased proportionally. Paradoxically, religion produced the industry and frugality that result in riches. As riches increased, so did pride, anger, and love of the world. The form of the religion remained while the spirit melted away. Wesley asked himself: "Is there no way to prevent this— this continual decay of pure religion?" He found that "we ought not to prevent people from being diligent and frugal; *we must exhort all Christians to gain all they can, and to save all they can, that is, in effect, to grow rich.*" [Weber's italics] [81]

Wesley suggested that those who gain all they can should consider giving all they can in order to increase in grace and in the knowledge of Christ, and lay up their treasures in heaven "where neither moth nor rust doth corrupt." [82]

The full economic effect of the great religious movements, whose significance in economic development lay mostly in their ascetic influence, appeared, as Wesley put it, only after the religious enthusiasm had waned. Along with Edward Dowden (1849–1913), Weber, the Irish poet and critic remarks that the urge "to make the most of both worlds" became dominant in the end. It was all right to make money as long as one made it legally. The man was blessed in a visible manner, and he could have the satisfaction of being favored of God. Furthermore, religious asceticism provided employers with sober, conscientious and industrious workers who felt that they were obeying the will of God.

This doctrine gave the Puritan the comforting assurance that the unequal distribution of the goods of this world was entirely due to the will of God. "For promotion cometh neither from the east, nor from the west, nor from the south. But God is the judge: He putteth down one, and setteth up another." [83] In the beginning, capitalism needed a labor force that was ready and willing to work very hard even for low wages. The idea of fulfillment of one's duty in a calling created workers prepared to work hard. The treatment of labor as a calling became as characteristic of the modern worker as the corresponding attitude toward acquisition of the businessman. In fact, Sir William Petty (1623–1687), an English political economist, attributed the economic power of Holland in the seventeenth century to the numerous dissenters who believed that labor and industry were their duty toward God.

In *The Protestant Ethic,* Weber advanced the thesis that

rational conduct on the basis of the idea of the calling was born from the spirit of Christian asceticism. He tried to demonstrate that the essential elements of the psychology of early capitalism were produced by Puritan worldly asceticism; even by the time of Ben Franklin the religious basis of this psychology had begun to disappear.

The Puritan wanted to work in a calling; today, he is compelled to do so. Once asceticism left the confines of the monastery and became part of everyday life, it not only influenced worldly morality but transformed it. It laid the foundation for the economic order that no individual can escape today.

As asceticism revolutionized the world, material goods not only increased, but began to control our lives. Religious asceticism gave birth to capitalism which no longer needs it. The idea of duty in one's calling prowls about in our lives like the ghost of dead religious beliefs. Weber's attempt to trace the influence of Protestant asceticism on modern culture has been carried forward by other men.

R. H. TAWNEY

Richard Harvey Tawney, the English economist, was born in India in 1880. He studied at Rugby and at Balliol College, Oxford, and taught at Glasgow University and Oxford University; before his recent death, he was Professor Emeritus of Economic History at the University of London. In his book, *Religion and the Rise of Capitalism,* Tawney poses questions such as:

> Has religious opinion in the past regarded questions of social organization and economic conduct as irrelevant to

the life of the spirit? Can religion admit the existence of
a sharp antithesis between personal morality and the practices which are permissible in business? Does the idea of
a church involve the acceptance of any particular standard
of social ethics, and, if so, ought a church to endeavor to
enforce it as among the obligations incumbent on its
members? [84]

Weber's theory of the influence of religion on social issues
led Tawney also to consider the issue. Weber felt that Christianity in the West, particularly certain varieties that had
acquired an independent life as a result of the Reformation,
had been more favorable to the rise of modern capitalism
than some of the other creeds. Tawney considered the remarks of Montesquieu who said that the English "had pro-
gressed furthest of all people in three important things, piety,
commerce and freedom." [85] Freedom had been attributed by
many to the influence of piety. In *The Protestant Ethic and
the Spirit of Capitalism,* Weber considered the debt commerce owed to piety.

Tawney dealt with the same subject matter as Weber, and
while respecting the points made by Weber, Tawney agreed
with the following criticism of Lujo Brentano, German
economist and author of the critique, *The Beginnings of
Modern Capitalism* [1916].

Weber, according to Tawney, seems to explain by reference
to moral and intellectual influence developments that have
their principal explanation in another area altogether. [86] In
the fifteenth century, the capitalist spirit flourished in Venice
and Florence, and in the south of Germany and Flanders—
the greatest commercial and financial centers of the time—
in spite of the fact that they were predominantly Catholic.

On the other hand, while there was a development of capitalism in Holland and England in the sixteenth and seventeenth
centuries, Brentano argued that this development was not
due to the fact that both countries were Protestant powers,
but rather to "large economic movements and in particular
to the discoveries and the results which flowed from them." [87]
Tawney maintains that it is somewhat artificial to imagine
that capitalistic enterprise could not possibly have appeared
without the influence of religious changes. It would be
equally true, and as one-sided, to assert that the religious
changes occurred only because of the economic movements.

Tawney investigated intellectual movements that Weber
largely ignored, ones that were favorable to economic relations though having little or nothing to do with religion.
Tawney agrees with Brentano that Venice and Florence rose
as economic, not religious, centers as a result of a Machiavel-
lian ethic. This ethic though was as powerful a solvent of
traditional ethical restraints as that of Calvin. Moreover,
speculations carried on by businessmen and economists were
instrumental in the promotion of single-minded concentration
on pecuniary gain which Tawney equates with Weber's capitalistic spirit.

Weber's entire treatment of Calvin seemed to Tawney to
be an oversimplification. The fact that Weber ascribes to
the English Puritans of the seventeenth century Calvinism's
concept of social ethics, and the fact that Weber refers to
the English Puritans as if they held more or less the same
beliefs on social ethics, as the Calvinists, Tawney regards as
misleading. The Puritans were firm believers in discipline
as, in general, were the Calvinists. The individualism ascribed
to them by Weber, especially to the Puritan movement in

its later phases, would have horrified them. Seventeenth-century Puritans held a variety of opinions regarding social policy, as Cromwell discovered when he tried to gather Puritan aristocrats and advocates of equality, landowners and diggers, merchants and artisans, soldiers and generals, into the fold of a unified social theory.

Tawney maintains that both the capitalist spirit and the Protestant ethic were far more complex than Weber considers them to be. While he concedes Weber's insistence that the commercial classes in seventeenth-century England were the standard-bearers of a particular concept of social ethics, Tawney contends that this was quite different from the principles of the more conservative elements in society—the peasants, craftsmen, and the landed gentry—and that this concept found expression in religion, politics, and in social as well as economic conduct and policy. Tawney was in agreement with John Maynard Keynes:

> "Modern capitalism, is absolutely irreligious without internal union, without much public spirit, often, though not always, a mere congeries of possessors and pursuers!" [and Tawney comments] . . . it is that whole system of appetites and values, with its deification of the life of snatching to hoard, and hoarding to snatch. . . . It was against that system, while its true nature was unknown even to itself, that the saints and sages of earlier ages launched their warnings and their denunciations.[88]

In his foreword to *The Protestant Ethic and the Spirit of Capitalism,* Tawney qualifies his acceptance of Weber's views:

> His [Weber's] conclusions are illuminating; but they are suspectible, it may perhaps be held, of more than one interpretation. There was action and reaction, and, while Puritanism helped to mould the social order, it was, in its

turn, moulded by it. It is instructive to trace, with Weber, the influence of religious ideas on economic development. It is not less important to grasp the effect of the economic arrangements accepted by an age on the opinion which it holds of the province of religion.[89]

WERNER SOMBART

The connection between religious ethics and the growth of capitalism also attracted Werner Sombart. Sombart's interest in the subject was, as Tawney's, aroused by Weber's *The Protestant Ethic*. Although agreeing with Weber on the possibility of religion's influence on economic change, Sombart asserted that capitalism was of Jewish origin.

In his book, *The Jews and Modern Capitalism,* Sombart dwelt on the influence of the Jews on the development of capitalism. The work may be divided into two parts. First, Sombart seeks to define the role played by the Jews in the formation of the modern economic system. The second part consists of examining the sociopsychological and moral forces in the Jewish religious ethic that prepared the Jews for the promotion of this new set of economic principles.

The latter problem is more fundamental. Unless it can be shown that elements in the culture of medieval Judaism were instrumental in making the Jews the originators of modern capitalism, collecting facts on Jewish participation in the financial enterprises of the early modern age serves no purpose in this discussion.

Sombart has had many critics, among them Dr. Bert F. Hoselitz. Although Sombart's work was evoked by Weber's hypothesis on the relation between the Puritan ethic and the growth of capitalism, Hoselitz took issue with Sombart's thesis that "those parts of the Puritan dogma which appear to be of real importance for the formation of the spirit of capitalism are borrowed from the realm of ideas of the Jewish religion." [90] Sombart's thesis is that the impersonal, rational, "materialistic commercialism" characteristic of the capitalistic spirit can be traced back to the Jewish religion and thought, as one of the indispensable sources.

Hoselitz points out that in his efforts to find elements favorable to the formation of the capitalistic spirit, Sombart examines various aspects of Jewish law and religion, and brings to bear, wherever appropriate, rules of behavior and tenets of conduct drawn from a multitude of sources. Hoselitz finds, at this point, that Sombart's knowledge of Hebrew and other sources is defective. Both the medieval Jews as well as the gentiles had an abundance of books on the subject of morality and good conduct. These books, according to Hoselitz, provide sufficient insight into the standards of conduct and, particularly, into the economic behavior of medieval Jewry. These works, argues Hoselitz, are totally ignored by Sombart who accepts only the canonical books of the Bible, the Talmud, and three medieval codes written by Maimonides (1135–1240), Asher ben Yechiel (1250–1327), and Joseph Caro (1488–1575). On the strength of this material, Sombart reaches the conclusion that the Jewish religion is essentially rationalistic and almost completely free from any mysticism. Hoselitz remarks that this view is untenable; not only does Sombart underestimate the profoundly mystical character of the Kabbalistic writings, he also misinterprets the deep penetration of mysticism in Chasidism. What justification is there, asks Hoselitz, for Sombart to attribute to the literate Jew who has learned to read and interpret the Talmud, a rationalism that is entirely foreign to him? Hoselitz finds a constant bias on Sombart's part in seeing a "rationalistic capitalist" wherever he looked. After all, the Jew does not believe in accepting the binding power of the law on a rational basis but on the basis of his faith in the truth of his religion. Hoselitz cites Julius Guttmann who does not tire of pointing out that mystical traits have been found in Judaism as early as Philo (30 B.C.–50 A.D.), Solomon ibn Gabirol (1021–1058), and Judah Halevi (1085-1140). Even today, evidence of Jewish mysticism may be found in Martin Buber who has influenced scores of Christian thinkers—among them Roman Catholic philosopher Jacques Maritain, Russian Orthodoxy's Nikolai Berdyaev, Protestantism's Karl Barth and Paul Tillich.

Frequently critics of Sombart accuse him of using only that part of the evidence that supports his thesis. Sombart's argument on the commercial acumen of the Jewish rabbis is based on a misunderstanding of the role of the rabbi in Jewish culture. The rabbi is not only a priest; he is also a teacher. Hoselitz points out that, as a teacher, the rabbi naturally familiarized himself with all aspects of law and the rules of daily commercial and personal intercourse of the members of his community. However, since the wisdom of the rabbi extended far beyond his knowledge of the rules of trade, the rabbi was appreciated not only for his knowledge of commerce, but for his understanding of other phases of life as well.

If, says Hoselitz, it is correct to regard the Jews as the transmitters of an ancient culture into more modern times, it must be equally true of the Arabs, the various monastic orders, and the citizens of Venice, Genoa and other Mediterranean towns who transmitted ancient economic concepts, some of which appear to resemble capitalist maxims. These were modified in modern times to suit the changing conditions. The prohibition in Jewish law of taking usury from one's brother was gradually relaxed among Jews, as well as among gentiles. Hoselitz regards this relaxation of the prohibition to take usury, in the face of opposing legal and religious sanctions, as being based not primarily on factors in Jewish law or commercial relations, but rather on the gradual development of economic relations that made the taking of interest an indispensable factor in the further growth of commerce and production.

Sombart's major thesis is that the shift of the commercial center of the Western world from the Mediterranean basin to Antwerp, and later to Holland, helped the countries to which the Jews migrated by their active participation and trade with the Levant, by their leadership in Dutch colonial enterprises, and in their role as money lenders and financial administrators to princes. Nevertheless, Hoselitz points out that although Jewish financiers in the late seventeenth and early eighteenth centuries contributed to the stability of several centralized territorial states, the fact of centralization and the elimination of prosperous and economically powerful free cities—which might challenge the princes—was accomplished in the sixteenth and early seventeenth centuries when the German princes depended not on the Jews but on the Christian merchants of Augsberg, Frankfurt, and Nuremberg.

Hoselitz also rejects Sombart's claim regarding the importance of the Jewish migration to Antwerp and Holland, the participation of the Jews in colonial enterprises, and the importance of the Jewish monopoly in the Levantine trade. He cites Grunwald's study showing that the Levantine trade of Holland in the seventeenth century did not exceed 3 percent of the total Dutch trade.

It is entirely possible that Sombart was influenced by external similarities between the Jewish destiny and the Christian merchants of Augsberg, Frankfurt, and Nuremberg. They lived almost all the time as a "pariah" people. Wherever the Jews migrated they were influenced by the changes surrounding them. By their migration from feudal Spain to "capitalist" Antwerp and Holland, Jewish personality patterns, states Hoselitz, changed. In a generation or two, the Jews developed the faculties that enabled them to carry on a successful existence in their new environment. Hoselitz, who wrote the introduction to the English edition of Sombart's book, concludes that it was not the Jews as they were that made capitalism, but rather it was capitalism that made the Jews what they were.

SUMMARY

To trace all of the developments out of and beyond Weber's *The Protestant Ethic,* would form a book in itself. The two earliest, most significant developments were those of Tawney and Sombart. Tawney proposed to modify Weber's thesis in one way (by tracing the emergence of a capitalistic psychology to roots deeper than the Protestant Reformation, and by adding nonreligious causes to its distinctive orientation) and Sombart in another (by substituting a Jewish for a Protestant origin to the distinctive psychology of capitalism which, as a Socialist, he despised). It may be noted that both

Tawney and Sombart accepted a major premise of Weber's thesis: neither doubted that religion (at least some religion) had played a significant role in the genesis of the spirit of capitalism. Except for neo-Marxian theorists, none of the later major commentators have rejected the thesis at this level. The majority have accepted this thesis along the lines indicated by Tawney: that, with modifications, Weber was essentially correct.

Following the lines of the Weber-Tawney thesis, this study presents a cross-cultural examination of religion and economic behavior as represented by the Quakers in the West, and the Jains of India.

NOTES

1. It is difficult to define "religion," for the term has a variety of meanings. Matthew Arnold says that religion is "morality touched with emotion," while Hegel holds that a genuine religion should be revealed and the revelation must come from God. Whitehead insists that religion is "what the individual does with his own solitariness." John McTaggart feels that, "religious attitude is a conviction of harmony between ourselves and the universe at large." H. J. Paton, *The Modern Predicament* (London, 1955), p. 59.

Ludwig Feuerbach in his *Critique of the Hegelian Philosophy* argues that "religion is the dream of the human mind." Yet this dream, he stated further, is not quite devoid of reality: "We see real things, but in the entrancing splendour of imagination and caprice instead of in the simple daylight of reality and necessity." John Passmore, *A Hundred Years of Philosophy* (London, 1957), p. 76. Caird thinks that religion must be studied historically and the proper question is never, "Is that religion true or false?" but rather, "How much truth has been brought to expression and with what inadequacies and unexplained assumptions?" Ibid., p. 54.

Bernard Bosanquet asserts that deeper and wider experiences —short of the Absolute—that possess real value are art, science, social participation, and religion which to him are the same as "absorption in a good." Ibid., p. 87. Friedrich Albert Lange says that man has no choice but to supplement reality by an ideal world of his own creation. Ibid., p. 98. Cardinal J. H. Newman in his *An Essay in Aid of a Grammar of Assent* (1870), speaking of religion, states that to approach it by means of demonstrative arguments is to take chemists for our cooks and minerologists for our masons. To Newman it is conscience and not demonstrative proof that leads men to God. Ibid., p. 100.

For purposes of the present study, these philosophic issues can be set aside: "religion" will be considered as being what society ordinarily designates by the term.

2. Max Weber, *The Protestant Ethic and the Spirit of Capitalism,* trans. Talcott Parsons (New York, 1958).

3. Max Weber, *The Religion of China,* trans. by Don Martindale (Glencoe, Ill., 1951). From this work by Weber, as pointed out by Bendix, Confucianism and Puritanism represent two comprehensive and mutually exclusive types of rationalism, each attempting an internally consistent, intellectual ordering of human life based upon certain ultimate religious beliefs. Both world views were compatible with the accumulation of wealth. However, they had different ends in view. The Confucian aimed at preserving a cultured status position. Wealth, thus, was the basis of dignity and self-perfection. Puritans, on the other hand, oriented their ascetic conduct to ends that were totally alien to the aesthetic values of Confucianism. "It was this difference in the prevailing mentality that contributed to an autonomous capitalist development in the West and the absence of a similar development in China." Reinhard Bendix, *Max Weber* (New York, 1962), p. 141.

4. Weber, *The Protestant Ethic*, p. 14.

5. Ibid., p. 15.

6. Ibid., p. 16.

7. Ibid., pp. 17, 18.

8. Ibid., p. 27.

9. Ibid., p. 39.

10. Ibid., p. 40.

11. Ibid., p. 44.

12. Ibid., p. 51.

13. Ibid., p. 54.

14. Ibid., p. 57.

15. Ibid., p. 60.

16. H. H. Gerth and C. Wright Mills, eds., *From Max Weber* (New York, 1958), p. 414.

17. Weber, *The Protestant Ethic*, p. 62.

18. H. Richard Niebuhr stated that modifications of primitive Calvinism resulted from its alliance with the middle class and the relaxation of its restrictive social ethics. Calvin was not inclined to abandon the medieval principle of the supremacy of the church over all the institutions, and of religion over the interests of an individual. Only in theory, the church continued to be regarded as the rightful arbiter of family morals. Niebuhr concluded by quoting Tawney: "So the Calvinism which 'had begun by being the very soul of authoritarian regimentation, ended by being the vehicle of an almost Utilitarian individualism.'" H. Richard Niebuhr, *The Social Sources of Denominationalism* (New York, 1960), pp. 98–104.

Calvinism was modified to acquire a more definitely middle-class character through the influence of humanism, rationalism, and nineteenth-century science. According to critics of Weber's thesis of the Calvinistic parentage of capitalism, such typical representatives of the bourgeois spirit as Franklin and Carnegie derived their social ethics from the Illumination rather than from the Reformation. The middle classes, according to Niebuhr, generally received this new influence quite unconsciously, "unaware of any antagonism between rationalism they absorbed in

education and business and the teachings of their churches." Ibid.,
p. 104.

19. Weber, *The Protestant Ethic,* p. 65.

20. Ibid., p. 68.

21. Ibid., p. 71.

22. Commenting upon the role of Calvinism in the development of capitalism, J. Milton Yinger stated: "One must not
forget the important ways in which Calvinism was molded to
fit the needs of the class who had found in it the possibilities
of the kind of religious sponsorship that they required in their
struggle for advancement." These classes would have advanced
in any event, said Yinger. In fact, Yinger asserted that "they
probably would have found a religious sponsor in any event.
Nevertheless, it is not unimportant that Calvin's formulations
appeared when and where they did. Without them, capitalism
would have evolved along somewhat different lines." J. Milton
Yinger, *Religion, Society and the Individual* (New York, 1957),
p. 537.

23. Weber, *The Protestant Ethic,* p. 78.

24. Ibid., p. 83.

25. Ibid., p. 84.

26. Ibid., p. 87.

27. Ibid., p. 90.

28. Ibid., p. 91.

29. Ibid.

30. Ibid., p. 95

31. Ibid., p. 97.

32. Loraine Boettner, *The Reformed Doctrine of Predestination* (Grand Rapids, Mich., 1954), p. 13.

33. Daniel 4:35.

34. John Calvin, *Institutes of the Christian Religion,* trans. by
Henry Beveridge, bk. 3, chap. 21, sec. 5, (Grand Rapids, Mich.,
1949).

35. Ibid., chap. 10, sec. A:2.

36. Ibid., chap. 5, sec. 6, "Providence."

37. As cited in Weber, *The Protestant Ethic,* p. 101. Weber's

source was Eibach's essay in *Theologische Studien und Kritiken* (1879).

38. Weber, *The Protestant Ethic,* p. 103.

39. S. Carruthers, *The Westminster Confession,* (Manchester, England, 1938), chap. 3, sec. 6.

40. Weber, *The Protestant Ethic,* pp. 103, 104.

41. E. H. Klotsche and J. Theodore Mueller, *The History of Christian Doctrine* (Burlington, Iowa, 1945), p. 237.

42. Weber, *The Protestant Ethic,* p. 105.

43. II Peter 1:10.

44. Boettner, *The Reformed Doctrine of Predestination,* p. 309.

45. Klotsche and Mueller, *History of Christian Doctrine,* p. 237.

46. Weber, *The Protestant Ethic,* p. 109.

47. Ibid., p. 110.

48. Calvin, *Institutes,* bk. 3, chap. 4, p. 40.

49. Weber, *The Protestant Ethic,* p. 111.

50. Philippians 4:8; II Thessalonians 3:12, 13.

51. Boettner, *The Reformed Doctrine of Predestination,* p. 258.

52. Philippians 2:12, 13.

53. Weber, *The Protestant Ethic,* p. 118.

54. Ibid., p. 121.

55. Ibid., p. 123.

56. Romans 8:28; Colossians 3:22, 23.

57. Colossians 3:18, 19, 20.

58. Weber, *The Protestant Ethic,* p. 124.

59. Ibid., p. 128.

60. Klotsche and Mueller, *History of Christian Doctrine,* p. 282.

61. Ibid., p. 284.

62. Ibid., p. 285.

63. Ibid., p. 304.

64. William R. Cannon, *The Theology of John Wesley* (New York, 1946), p. 80.

65. Ephesians 5:27.

66. Weber, *The Protestant Ethic,* p. 147.

67. Ibid., p. 148.

68. Ibid., p. 150.

69. H. Richard Niebuhr, *The Social Sources of Denomina-tionalism* (New York, 1960), p. 20.

70. Weber, *The Protestant Ethic,* p. 155.

71. Matthew 12:36.

72. II Thessalonians 3:10, 12.

73. Genesis 1:28.

74. Weber, *The Protestant Ethic,* p. 162.

75. Matthew 25:29.

76. Proverbs 3:10; Job 42:12.

77. Deuteronomy 28:5, 12.

78. Weber, *The Protestant Ethic,* p. 166.

79. Ibid., p. 169.

80. Ibid., p. 172.

81. Ibid., p. 175. Weber's source was Southey, *Life of Wesley,* vol. 2, chap. 29, p. 308.

82. Matthew 6:19.

83. Psalms 75:6, 7.

84. R. H. Tawney, *Religion and the Rise of Capitalism* (New York, 1926), p. 286.

85. Ibid.

86. Tawney states that since there is a natural greed of gain, the existing evils of unscrupulous commercialism inevitably left some trace on the writings of Zwingli and possibly others. Zwingli for instance, insisted on the oft repeated thesis that private property originates in sin. In the case of Calvin, an English divine said that Calvin "deals with usurie as the apothecarie doth with poyson." Tawney draws attention to the fact that Calvin was very cautious in his economic reflections and merely wished to protect the borrower from high interests. The interpretation that Calvin meant that the debtor might properly be asked to concede some small part of his profits to the creditor with whose capital they had been earned has been misconstrued by some to mean that "the creditor becomes rich by the sweat of the debtor,

and the debtor does not reap the reward of his labor." Tawney
also feels that Calvin was not particularly original in his contribution to the theory of usury. In his sanction of a moderate
rate on loans to the rich, his position coincided with that of
Melanchthon. Ibid., pp. 94, 95.

Tawney further regards Calvinistic social ethics as erected on
a practical basis of urban industry and commercial enterprise.
"Upon their theological background," said Tawney, "it would
be audacious to enter." Tawney asserts that in the struggle
between liberty and authority, Calvinism sacrificed liberty, not
with reluctance, but with enthusiasm. "Most tyrannies have contented themselves with tormenting the poor. Calvinism had
little pity for the poverty; but it distrusted wealth . . . it did
its best to make life unbearable for the rich." Ibid., p. 115.

87. Ibid., p. 262.

88. Ibid., p. 286.

89. Weber, *The Protestant Ethic,* p. 10.

90. Werner Sombart, *The Jews and Modern Capitalism* (New
York, 1962), p. 12.

PART TWO

THE
QUAKERS OF
THE WEST

2

A SHORT HISTORY OF QUAKERISM

THE FOUNDER OF QUAKERISM

The founder of Quakerism, George Fox, was born in 1624. His life covers a period in English history that was dominated by Puritanism—a time in which men and women were agitated with questions as to the correct form of church, government, and worship. They were not pleased with a mechanically interpreted Scripture that operated as an external authority in matters of faith and practice. Many were attracted by a more mystical form of religion.

Though George Fox was not well educated, he was "dissatisfied with the teachings and practices of the day and longed for a higher and more spiritual life." [1] Fox worked as a cobbler from the age of fourteen until 1642 when he came under the influence of the ministry of Nathaniel Stephens, an Oxford graduate. Stephens, who was deeply grounded in Calvinistic theology, left a deep impression on

Fox. Fox knew his Bible very well. Although Fox had several relatives who were Baptists, Elbert Russell says that after Fox left home at the age of nineteen, he consulted various priests of the established church and many dissenters who had reputations for unusual religious beliefs or experiences. He soon acquired a practical knowledge of the history, beliefs, and practices of the English Protestant sects.[2]

Like the pilgrim in John Bunyan's *Grace Abounding,* and Gautama Buddha, the founder of Buddhism, Fox at the age of nineteen began a four-year pilgrimage as a seeker. According to the Quaker historian Emilia Fogelklou, unlike many of the other Puritans who were burdened with a sense of personal sin, Fox's spiritual problem was created by the disparity between the professions of his Puritan neighbors and their daily lives.[3] Two additional causes of Fox's spiritual depression, according to Russell, were the civil war between Parliament and King Charles I, which had been in progress for a year, and the lot of the underprivileged. It was difficult for Fox to reconcile the king's claim to the divine right of kings, and the professed religious aims and zeal of the Puritans with the brutalities and passions of warfare. This contradiction had such a profound effect on Fox that he decided to obliterate from his nature everything warlike. The sufferings of humanity moved him deeply and made him aware of the spiritual burden and the condition of all men in the world. Fox came to sympathize with all people; he brooded over the sorrow of the slave, those who labored and, as Russell says, those who suffered for conscience' sake.[4]

Calvinism itself also had a profound effect on Fox. Its joylessness produced in him a deep sense of sadness. Fox found no consolation in the doctrine of predestination, no matter how many commentaries lauded its virtues. Calvinism seemed to have a message for the elect only, and they were few in number. Russell says that it was "from this ocean of darkness of Calvinistic pessimism that Fox was seeking a way of escape."

Fox longed for direct access to God. He was dissatisfied with the priests with whom he came in contact; they were unable to satisfy him with their answers to the problems of physical and social ills that Fox saw all around him. Russell says: "At best they offered him substitutes for the knowledge of God; theological notions about God instead of vital faith, the mediation of a church whose rites and orders were established centuries before by a Christ who once lived on earth but was no longer accessible to men." [5] Even the Bible, which records that people heard the voice of the Spirit, had ceased to satisfy Fox.

Failing to find spiritual truth and genuine peace in the churches of his time and rejecting ecclesiastical doctrines as prior conditions of access to God, Fox, nevertheless, found truth and peace in a personal, intimate relationship with Christ. He said: "When all my hopes [in churches and churchmen] were gone, so that I had nothing outwardly to help me . . . then, I heard a voice which said, 'There is one, even Christ Jesus, that can speak to thy condition,' and when I heard it, my heart did leap for joy." [6]

His biographer, Russell, says that to the Puritan faith in God's omnipotence, Fox joined the concept that God is love and truth; he believed that those who open their lives fully to God may continue to live in that power "that is over all." Fox believed that such religious possibilities are in *all* men, and that this grace is for all—regardless of class, nation or geography.[7]

Fox was a nonconformist, believing in the separation of

church and state. He was also a reformer, always concerned
with the needs of men around him. His method of following
the Inward Light was well adapted to serve as the basis of a
religious society with a common life. At all times, Fox insisted on honesty and truthfulness. He renounced oaths, and
believed in the one-price system in trade, and just wages for
working people. Russell regards him as the creative personality in the Quaker movement who set the pattern for its
particular type of experience and its fundamental ideas. Fox
preached ceaselessly in Great Britain and in America. According to Neave Brayshaw, a biographer of George Fox, he was
imprisoned eight times for an aggregate of six years, including a brief confinement at Nottingham, a year in Derby jail,
nine months in the foul dungeon of Launceston jail, and
nearly a total of three years in Lancaster and Scarborough
castles.[8]

Fox influenced men from all walks of life, including
Robert Barclay, William Penn, and Issac Pennington. William
Penn has recorded his impression of Fox in the following
words:

> And truly, I must say, that though God had visibly clothed
> him with a divine preference and authority, and indeed
> his very presence expressed a religious majesty, yet he
> never abused it; but held his place in the church of God
> with great meekness, and a most engaging humility and
> moderation. For upon all occasions like his blessed Master,
> he was servant to all; holding and exercising his elder-
> ship, in the visible power that had gathered them, with
> reverence to the Head and care over the body; and was
> received only in that spirit and power of Christ as the first
> and chief elder of this age; who, as he was therefore
> worthy of double honor, so for the same reason it was

given by the faithful of the day; because his authority was inward and not outward, and that he got it and kept it by the love of God, and power of an endless life. . . .

He was of an innocent life, no busybody nor self-seeker, neither touchy nor critical; what fell from him was very inoffensive if not very edifying. So meek, contented, modest, easy, steady, tender, it was a pleasure to be in his company. He exercised no authority but over evil, and that every-where and in all; but with love, compassion, and long suffering. A most merciful man, as ready to forgive, as unapt to take offence. Thousands can truly say, he was of an excellent spirit and savor among them, and because thereof, the most excellent spirits loved him with an un-feigned and unfading love.[9]

THE BEGINNINGS
OF THE QUAKER MOVEMENT

From 1647, Fox began to propagate his new beliefs. During the next three years, Fox found receptive persons among the Baptists, Independents, Ranters and other sects in Notting-hamshire, Leicestershire, and Derbyshire, especially those near Mansfield.[10] Those who accepted the teachings of Fox called themselves by various names: Children of Truth, Children of Light, Friends of Truth, Friends, and Religious Society of Friends. Quakerism was undoubtedly revolutionary and was regarded as such by the established Church of England. The new converts were persecuted: from 1650 to 1689, more than 3,500 suffered for their faith; about 400 died in prison. Fox was jailed not only because he often spoke after the church service, but also because he interrupted the preacher during the sermon. Fox and his early followers refused to attend the services of the established church; they

insisted upon freedom of speech, assembly, and worship;
they refused to take oaths in the courts, and would not even
doff their hats to those they met in the streets, whether com-
moner or king. It is recorded that they made no distinctions
among people in sex or social class.

Fox traveled extensively in the northern counties of
England between 1651 and 1654; with his co-laborers, he
spread the message to other parts of England, especially
London and Bristol. It later spread to Wales, Ireland, the
Continent, and finally to America. When Fox died, there
were 50,000 Quakers.

Mary Fisher and Ann Austin, who were early leaders of
Quakerism, were already in America, having arrived in
Massachusetts in 1656 from Barbados. Rhode Island became
an asylum for people of all beliefs and the women secured a
stronghold there. Quakerism, through the efforts of its missionaries, spread to France, although the Catholic countries
remained almost untouched by the Quaker influence, despite
the activities of ardent missionaries. Initially those Quakers
who came to America came as missionaries; many of them
were women who often suffered persecution for preaching in
the streets. Ann Austin and Mary Fisher were accused of
being witches and deported. Between 1655 and 1670, the
number of Quaker missionaries who left England for America
increased. Apart from Rhode Island, they met with hostile
treatment wherever they went.

According to the Quaker historian A. Thomas, the earliest
monthly meeting in America was established at Sandwich,
Massachusetts.[11] Roger Williams disagreed with the Puritan
authorities in Massachusetts, contending that the civil government had no authority over the consciences of men. He also

insisted that payment be made to the American Indians for the land confiscated. Any person who claimed to be regenerate should be exempted from taking an oath which he interpreted as a form of worship. After being banished from Massachusetts, Williams settled at Providence, Rhode Island. He secured a charter in 1644 and again in 1651. This colony was used as an asylum for the refugees who fled the persecution of the Puritan colonies and England.[12]

Ann Hutchinson, a leader of a controversy with the Massachusetts authorities, found herself exiled, along with her sympathizers, to Rhode Island. Some Quakers were stripped and subjected to outrageous examination for marks of witches. Boston authorities forbad any shipmaster to bring Quakers into the colony. Any Quakers who did arrive were whipped, imprisoned, isolated from others, and finally banished. If a Quaker returned after banishment, his right ear was cut off.

In spite of persecution, the Quaker movement continued to grow and many new converts were added. Long after the Restoration in England, religious toleration was established in at least some of the colonies in America. With the death of George Fox and the passage of the Toleration Act of 1689 in England, a new phase opened. Quakers found themselves persecuted less and less, but they also found their zeal diminishing. Frank S. Mead states:

> They settled down, looked within rather than without, and began enforcing discipline on their membership so strictly that they became in fact a "peculiar people." Members were disowned for even minor infractions of the discipline; thousands were cut off for "marrying out of Meeting." Pleasure, music, and art were taboo; sobriety, punctuality, and honesty were demanded in all directions; dress was painfully plain, and speech was Biblical. They were different

and dour; they gained few new converts and lost many old members.[13]

Indeed, the Quakers were treated as an outcast minority. However, they organized themselves. Emphasis was placed on a closely knit family life. The separatist and semi-ascetic attitude toward those outside the group was reinforced by the loyalty that persecution nurtured. Mystical experience with the divine was stressed. In fact, it was a requirement prior to becoming a member of the fellowship. The Quakers had, at the beginning, all the characteristics of a typical sect. H. Richard Niebuhr says:

> A church is socially obligatory, the necessary consequence of birth into a family or nation, and no special requirements condition its privileges; the institutional church attaches a high importance to the means of grace which it administers, to the system of doctrine which it has formulated, and to the official administration of sacraments and teaching by an official clergy. . . . The sect on the other hand attached primary importance to the religious experience of its members prior to fellowship with the group . . . frequently rejects an official clergy, preferring to trust for guidance to lay inspiration rather than to theology or liturgical expertness. . . . By the very nature of its constitution it [the church] is committed to the accommodation of its ethics of civilization; it must represent the morality of the respectable majority, not of the heroic minority.[14]

The early period of withdrawal proved to be a time of cultural creativity and mystical inwardness. The Quakers became philanthropists, took an active part in prison reforms, and established educational institutions. They treated the American Indians like human beings and it is recorded that the Indians responded well to this treatment. They tried to abolish slavery because it violated the Golden Rule. Niebuhr refers to the Quakers as one of the churches of the disinherited because, even more than the Anabaptists, they continued to represent the social idealism of these churches. Equality was symbolized by the use of "thee" and "thou"; their continual support of humanitarian activities represented an effective continuation of democratic ethics. Niebuhr points out that because of the rejection of a religion of the disinherited, a new denomination once more arose. This was inevitable; as Weber and Niebuhr have stated, some periods of Christian history were strongly influenced by the interests of the middle class, and many modern organizations had their sources as separate organizations in their own interests, rather than in the interests of common humanity. Eventually, the churches of the poor, as a result of much diligence, took their place alongside other denominations. At this juncture, one may add Weber's contention that the godliness of the poor also served to bring about their simultaneous economic success. In the second and third generations, the Quakers became more or less a respectable middle-class church that left the popular movement from which it originated far behind.

In spite of being pacifistic in their attitude, a few did take part in the American Revolution; most, however, worked quietly for peace. In some instances a few permitted slavery; however, Quakers had rid their society of slavery long before the rest of the members of any other religious body in America. After the Civil War, an active part was taken by the Quakers in the education and legislative protection of the free Negro.

There is no Protestant denomination that has not had some division among its members. Quakers are no exception; the Hicksites separated in 1827, the Wilburites in 1845, and the Primitives in 1861. Other separations were the North Carolina Society in 1904, and one in Iowa in 1887. Frank Mead states that the twentieth century has been a century of Quaker unity and growth. A large proportion of the pastoral meetings have been merged into what is known as the Five-Years Meeting, which was organized in 1902. Those that parted company in 1827 (the two Philadelphia meetings) have been meeting in joint sessions, as have the two New York yearly meetings.[15]

THE FAITH OF THE QUAKERS: THEIR RELIGIOUS DOCTRINES

It is difficult to divorce the religious doctrines of the Quakers from their ethical practices for the two are closely intertwined. However, an attempt will be made to do so.

Many sects have come into existence because they have been dissatisfied with prevailing religious teachings and practices. Although the Quakers accepted the ascetic ideals and practices of the Puritans, they wished to augment and purify the Puritan doctrines. Their opposition to all outward authority in religion was a radical break with historical Christianity. They have no theological language and no formal creed or confession of binding authority. The writings of Robert Barclay the Apologist (1648–1690), and his Catechism of 1673, along with the writings of William Penn and George Fox, are regarded as authoritative by the faithful.

Klotsche and Mueller state that Fox and his followers did

not aim at an outward organization, but that gradually a form
of church government modeled somewhat after the Presbyterian system came into being. Among the Quakers, the
separate congregations or "particular meetings" are grouped
into superior meetings known as "monthly," "quarterly," and
"yearly"; these act as the executive of the society, including in
their supervision matters of spiritual discipline and secular
policy. The yearly meeting is the body of final authority.[16]
According to Mead, group decisions await the "sense of the
meeting." If lack of unity exists in the meeting, this is
resolved by having a "quiet time" for a few minutes until
unity is found, or it may postpone consideration of the matter
or refer it to a committee for study. Unlike other organizations, those who are in the minority are not outvoted but
convinced. Men, women, and children are at liberty to speak
in any meeting; the delegates who are appointed at quarterly
and yearly meetings to ensure adequate representation, do not
enjoy any unusual position or prerogative. Women are regarded with absolute equality in Quaker policy.[17] While the
elders are selected for their spiritual leadership, they stand
on an equal footing with the rest of the members of the congregation. Modest salaries are paid those working as full-time
ministers.

Whether the worship is formal, as in a Protestant service,
or informal, with no set pattern or program, there are no
outward rites or sacraments. The manner of Quaker worship
falls in a category between Catholicism and Protestantism.
The Quaker service is strictly subjective and places no dependence on the vicarious offices of any human minister. The
individual is expected to achieve a mystical union with the
divine. Barclay said: "When I came into the silent assemblies

of God's people, I felt a secret power among them, and as I gave way unto it, I found the evil weakening in me, and the good raised up." Thomas R. Kelly (1893–1941), Quaker social worker and professor of philosophy, said: "In a truly covered meeting an individual who speaks takes no credit to himself for the part he played in the unfolding of the worship. In fact he deeply regrets it if anyone, after the service, speaks in complimentary fashion to him." [18]

The very form of Quaker worship makes clear, more than any particular doctrine, that what is held in highest esteem is the place of mysticism in the life of each individual. Although great importance is placed on the Bible, the Spirit of God that produced the Bible is given preeminence. Among non-Quakers there is a tendency for orthodox groups to accept the Bible as the final authority in all religious matters, whereas among the Quakers it is the modern liberals who are drawn to the authority of the Bible.

Quakers find religion to be most compelling when it is reduced to its simplest terms—the love of God and one's neighbor. It will be profitable to consider briefly the Quaker position on the relation of man to God, the nature of good and evil, soteriology and eschatology. It is somewhat difficult to state the Quaker position clearly on these varied subjects since most of the literature is devoted to the subject of the Inner Light or mysticism. The individual is permitted a wide latitude on doctrinal issues.

William Wistar Comfort, a contemporary chronicler of the Quaker movement, remarks, however:

> The Quakers belong historically to the Puritan movement, [but] because of their disparagement of the world's charms, they are at the opposite pole from the Presbyterians in their

manner of conducting the fight against sin. The Quaker exercises silent pressure against the evil he sees about him; the Puritan takes up carnal weapons against the devil and all his works.[19]

Mysticism

Essentially, Quakerism is a mystical interpretation of Christianity. Generally, a mystic claims direct awareness of God —even consciousness of union with Him. After having spent years in vain searching for the truth, George Fox had a mystical experience; when no outward help was left, he discovered that Christ alone could speak to his heart. This inward experience of realizing the consciousness of Christ has become, for the Quaker movement, the most fundamental of all its tenets. The mystic experience is not limited to any particular religion or country; it has been given prominence among Catholics, Protestants, Jews, Hindus, Buddhists, Jains and numerous other sects. No definition of religious mysticism in general abstract terms is ever satisfactory—not even for the Quaker. Rufus Jones, who has been considered the foremost spokesman for the Quaker movement, says:

> There are all possible stages and degrees of the experience of this "relation" from simple awareness of the soul's Divine Companion to rapt consciousness of union with the One and Only Reality. The term mystical is properly used for any type of religion which insists upon an immediate inward revelation of God within the sphere of personal experience. The person who has found within the deeps of himself the bubbling streams from the Eternal Fountain of Life, and no longer feels compelled to go back to the pools of tradition or the stagnant wells of authority for his supplies, the person who feels in himself the pulsation of That which Is, and feels as directly sure of God as he

is of his own personality, has in so far a mystical religion, though he may have no ecstasies, and may keep a sane and normal hold upon the finite and the visible . . . [The special form which such experiences take depends largely upon the peculiar type of psychical constitution which the person possesses.] [20]

Since the beginning of Quakerism, the mystic experience has been given prime importance, the Inner Light being far more important than any theological propositions. Calvinism had a precise doctrine of salvation; Quakerism does not possess any doctrine as such, but rather relies on the *experience* of the individual as the means of achieving grace. Instead of the theological tenets of Puritanism, the experience of new birth was achieved by the inward revelation: "That which is born of the Spirit is spirit. . . . The wind bloweth where it listeth, and thou hearest the sound thereof, but canst not tell whence it cometh, and whither it goeth: so is every one that is born of the Spirit." [21] Because of the immediate influence of Calvinism, many apologists, including Barclay, tried to develop a theory of the divinely sent substitute who was to redeem mankind. Later, Quakers stressed the point that God loves all sinners, including the prodigal. God is love; therefore, He is anxious to speak to every man. How God saves is not as important as the fact that He does save. Subsequent Quakers have deplored the early attempts to find suitable answers to difficult theological questions. It is love that answers all questions.

Sacraments

Along with a disdain for theological arguments, the Quakers place little importance on the sacraments. For centuries, both baptism and the Lord's Supper had caused much conflict and division in the Christian churches. The early Quakers were not unaware of the discussions of Luther, Zwingli, and others on these subjects. Charles M. Woodman remarks: "In its place they attempted to live the Sacrament in their relations with their fellow men. In other words, all life and, hence, all human conduct were sacraments. No higher ideal for human action had ever been set." [22] There have been instances when attempts have been made to have baptismal services as well as the Lord's Supper. These, however, have been regarded as erroneous, and not in the best Quaker tradition.

Revelation

Two important doctrines held by the Quakers are the Universal Light and Immediate Revelation. Both are based on the text found in John 1:9: "That was the true Light, which lighteth every man that cometh into the world." While Calvinistic doctrines have unconsciously permeated the Quaker teaching, an attempt is made constantly to keep them in the background. The fundamentalist's literal interpretation is not acceptable to the Quakers. Revelation is not limited to the Bible; God has not spoken once and for all, but is capable and does speak to men and women in this day and age. The doctrine of Universal Light coupled with the doctrine of the Immediate Revelation means that any man who wishes to listen to the voice of God may do so. It is possible for the most humble human being, however weak, to enjoy this privilege. The Bible is not to be entirely rejected, but must be interpreted according to the changing conditions that prevail. The Bible contains a progressive revelation that continues on to the present through the Inner Light an individual receives in his heart.

Certain people have been considered as channels of the

divine revelation: George Fox, Robert Barclay and, in this century, Rufus Jones. Through an understanding of Christ, man understands God. Christ is regarded as the One who arouses the kind of faith and wonder that inspires men to revitalize their lives. Christ has brought the unfolding of the eternal gospel, the revelation of God. Truth then, as Jones puts it, "is not a logical judgment, or a spoken message, or a transmitted idea; it is something that a person can be." [23] This is the purpose of revelation in man—to reveal Christ— but without theological predicaments to cloud the discovery of Christ, which moves a true Quaker to live the life of Christ on earth.

Immortality

The Quakers have a positive belief in eternal life. The New Testament idea, as revealed by Paul and others, regarding the hereafter is accepted. No dogmatic claim is made as to the precise meaning of eternal life; it is simply regarded as a hope for all believers. Through rediscovery of moral and spiritual grandeur, faith in immortality is said to be reinforced. Immortality is not bestowed merely because one desires it, but rather rests upon the moral consistency of the universe and upon the trustworthy character of the eternal nature of things. Rufus Jones remarks:

> Life as Jesus uses it, means life in its eternal or absolute sense. "Eternal" is not to be taken primarily in a quantitative sense, to signify mere endlessness. It is rather a life of new dimensions, life raised to new capacities—the full opening out of life Godward. By a birth from above, the soul partakes of the Life of God and enters upon a type of life as inexhaustible as His life is and as incapable of being ended by physical catastrophes.[24]

NOTES

1. E. H. Klotsche and J. Theodore Mueller, *The History of Christian Doctrine* (Burlington, Iowa, 1945), p. 293.

2. Elbert Russell, *The History of Quakerism* (New York, 1943), p. 19.

3. Emilia Fogelklou and James Nayler, *The Rebel Saint,* trans. Lajla Yapp (London, 1931), p. 45, 46.

4. Russell, *History of Quakerism,* p. 21.

5. Ibid., p. 22.

6. Ibid., p. 11.

7. Ibid., p. 24.

8. A. Neave Brayshaw, *The Personality of George Fox* (London, 1933), p. 59.

9. George Fox, *A Journal or Historical Account of the Life of George Fox,* bicentenary ed. (London, 1891), pp. iii–ix.

10. Russell, *History of Quakerism,* p. 19.

11. A. Thomas, *A History of Friends in America,* 6th ed. (Philadelphia, 1930), p. 69.

12. Russell, *History of Quakerism,* p. 40.

13. Frank S. Mead, *Handbook of Denominations in the United States* (Nashville, 1956), p. 106.

14. H. Richard Niebuhr, *The Social Sources of Denominationalism* (New York, 1960), p. 18.

15. Mead, *Handbook of Denominations,* p. 107.

16. Klotsche and Mueller, *History of Christian Doctrine,* p. 293.

17. Mead, *Handbook of Denominations,* p. 108.

18. William Wistar Comfort, *Quakers in the Modern World* (New York, 1949), p. 100.

19. Ibid., p. 71.

20. William C. Braithwaite, *The Beginnings of Quakerism* (New York, 1912), pp. xxxiv–xxxv.

21. John 3:6, 8.

22. Charles M. Woodman, *Quakers Find a Way* (Indianapolis, 1950), p. 78.

23. Harry Emerson Fosdick, *Rufus Jones Speaks to Our Time* (New York, 1954), p. 45.

24. Ibid., p. 286.

3

EVERYDAY
ETHIC OF
QUAKERISM

The code or set of principles by which men live, often referred to as ethics, is never purely academic. In the past, the
Quakers had a particular set of principles that guided their
daily conduct. Non-Quakers often regarded them as a peculiar
people because of their speech, their refusal to take oaths,
their manner of worship, the way they made decisions, the
clothing they wore, their attitude toward war, and the way
they carried on their business meetings. Charles M. Woodman
remarks:

> The main reason for all these differences is to be found in
> the Quaker estimate of man as man before his fellowmen
> and before his God. It may be expressed in a twofold
> statement: first, that all men are equal with all other men,
> and second, that all men come immediately into the presence
> of God and need no human being to represent them before
> their Father who is in heaven.[1]

As a way of life, Quakerism is not merely mysticism, but

group mysticism, primarily directed toward the inner life. An individual is expected to walk each step of the way according to the light within him. "If we walk in the light, as He is in the light, we have fellowship one with another." [2] If the individual walks according to this Inner Light, he will be in possession of the truth. "The anointing . . . abideth in you, and ye need not that any man teach you: but as the same anointing teacheth you of all things, and is truth . . . even as it hath taught you, ye shall abide in Him." [3]

THE QUAKER WORSHIP

The Quaker is interested in directing his daily life in accordance with the Inner Light and fellowship with others. Brinton says that "as Catholic worship is centered in the altar and Protestant worship in the sermon, worship for the Society of Friends attempts to realize as its center the divine Presence revealed within." [4] There is no pulpit or altar. The worshipper is expected to be in touch with the divine through the Inner Light; only beginners are given any guidance, for mature Quakers are expected to receive it on their own. No expensive edifice is ever constructed. Worship is considered by the faithful to be the most serious business of life. While a Quaker preacher may be present at the meeting, it is not essential to have one. Moreover, Quaker ministers are not ordained but are merely recognized, and preaching is not limited to those recognized.

All those present at a meeting have the responsibility of waiting upon the Lord for a message. If one receives a definite urge from the Inner Light to pass on a message, he may do so. The message may be very short. No set day such as Sunday is considered particularly important for a meeting. The day chosen is one that is convenient. Three generations ago there were no bells to beckon the worshippers to the worship service, for no bells were needed to remind them to worship the Lord. Men and women removed their hats before speaking in the meetings: "If a woman is about to speak one can feel the inspiration moving within her, for she has lifted her hands to untie the strings of her Quaker bonnet, preparatory to taking it off while she delivers the message which has been given her in the midst of the silence." [5] Quite often, absolutely not a word is spoken. Only among the youth meetings do the Friends permit hymn singing. The Nonpastoral groups do not use hymns in the regular meetings for worship.

Charles Lamb's classic words indicate what the Quaker receives from this peculiar worship meeting:

> Would'st thou know what true peace and quiet mean; would'st thou find a refuge from the noises and clamours of the multitude; would'st thou possess the depth of thine own spirit in stillness, without being shut out from the consolatory faces of thy species; would'st thou be alone, and yet accompanied; solitary, yet not desolate; singular, yet not without some to keep thee in countenance; a unit in aggregate; a simple in composite:—come with me into a Quakers' Meeting. . . .
>
> Retire with me into a Quakers' Meeting. . . . O, when the spirit is sore fretted, even tired to sickness of the janglings, and nonsense-noises of the world, what a balm and a solace it is to go and seat yourself for a quiet half-hour upon some undisputed corner of a bench, among the gentle Quakers! [6]

The Quaker cultivates inward detachment from the world. From about 1700 to 1850, especially during the period from

1800 to 1850, Quakers were referred to as quietists. "Quiet-ism is the doctrine that every self-centered trait or activity must be supressed or quieted in order that the divine may find unopposed entrance to the soul." [7] The Quakers, thus, learn in the meetings to "empty" themselves, surrender themselves, deny themselves, even while engaging in overt activities. It is the Quaker way of "obeying Him whose service is true liberty."

THE QUAKER COSTUME

In Britain, the early Quakers objected to the expensive, gaudy clothing worn by members of the royal family. Fox approved only of apparel of the simplest kind. Eventually simplicity of dress was observed by all the Quakers. In the Quaker "queries" or questions—a regular feature of the Quaker meetings—color, style, and material used in clothing were carefully regulated; those unwilling to comply were disciplined.

According to Woodman and other Quaker historians, simplicity of dress became a kind of honorary badge of membership, a testimony of distinctness from the rest of the world. Quakers were exhorted to avoid pride and immodesty in apparel and extravagant wigs, as well as all other vain and superfluous fashions of the world. William Penn said: "Choose thy clothes by thine eyes, not another's. The more plain and simple they are, the better: neither unshapely, nor fantastical; and for use and decency, and not for pride." [8]

Woodman observes that those possessed of ample means clothed themselves in Quaker garb, but they made up in quality of material and tailoring for what they lacked in ostentatiousness. Some young people were in this manner able to "show off." Being born into a Quaker family did not automatically give young people a desire to wear simple clothes. A story is told of Elizabeth Guerney and her brother, Joseph John, who were from a good Quaker family in Norwich, London. Both obliged their parents by attending the meetings regularly, although Elizabeth kept a diary in which she recorded her displeasure with them. However, one day she was converted and, leaving all the gay clothing aside, she became a good Quaker. In the service of Quaker causes she helped to bring about prison reform. Joseph too, although fond of gaudy apparel, was converted and gave up his worldly garb. As a decided Quaker, he became an evangelist.[9] Guerney became an influential Quaker doing perhaps more to shape modern Quakerism than any other individual. The Quaker garb symbolizes a way of life and has served as a continual reminder to the Quaker to act in a manner in his daily life which would bring glory to his God.

THE LANGUAGE OF THE QUAKERS

Quakers not only wore plain and simple clothes, but in their speech attempted to do away with the "evils of a class system" which required the use of "you" to superiors. The use of the singular pronouns "thou" and "thee" was customary with the Quakers from the very beginning. Originally, however, they consented to use "Your Honor" or "Your Highness" when addressing the nobility.

Since all men are equal in the sight of God, the Quakers considered it unnecessary to set up superficial distinctions. Woodman mentions an incident in the life of young Thomas

Ellwood, a stalwart first-generation Quaker who saw "the light" and wished to do his part in protesting the evils of the class system by using the familiar thou and thee. One day he used this form of speech before his father, who was also the magistrate. His father warned him, "Sirrah, if I ever hear you say 'thou' or 'thee' to me again, I'll strike your teeth down your throat." [10]

George Fox even disapproved of the names for the days. Sunday was named after the Sun god; Tuesday was derived from Zeus; Wednesday derived from Woden; Thursday was the god of thunder, Thor; Friday was the name of a goddess, the wife of Woden; Saturday was derived from the god Saturn. Woodman mentions that for these reasons Fox instructed his followers to refer to the days of the week as the first day, second day, etc., after the biblical account of creation in Genesis, 1:5–"There was evening and there was morning, one day." Similarly, appropriate changes were made in the names of the months. The orthodox Quakers changed the popular jingle, "Thirty days hath September,/April, June, and November . . ." to read:

> The fourth, eleventh, ninth and sixth,
> We thirty days to each affix;
> All the rest have thirty-one
> Except the second month alone;
> to it we twenty-eight assign;
> But leap year makes it twenty-nine.

In this day, it is not easy to use language this plain. Orthodox Quakers avoid addressing other Quakers as Mr., Mrs., and Miss by using their first names alone; in the case of young persons addressing those who are older, full names are employed: thus, "Jack Smith, I am glad to see thee looking well." Comfort remarks that there is some inconsistency found among the present-day Friends. They do not hesitate employing such titles as Doctor, Professor, and President.[11] Further, trivial words and expressions such as "luck," "chance," and "I'll bet," were not heard two generations ago. "Goodbye," being the same as "God be with you," was replaced by "farewell" since one should not take the name of the Lord lightly.

The opposition of the Quakers to taking oaths is well known. Many a Quaker has suffered for his conscience. In the memoirs of John Roberts (1620–1683), one reads how Roberts' son, Daniel, was once detained by Sir Thomas Cutter who asked him:

> "What's your name?"
> "Daniel Roberts."
> "Can you swear?"
> "Not that I know of; I never tried."
> "Then you must begin now."
> "I think I shall not."
> "How will you help it?"
> "By not doing it. But if thou canst convince me by that book in thy hand [the Bible] that it is lawful to swear, since Christ forbids it, then I will swear. For when men come and say, 'you must swear or suffer,' tis but reasonable to expect such men should be qualified to prove it lawful. Our Saviour says 'swear not at all,' thou sayest I must swear. Pray which must I obey?"
> "Well, Daniel, if you will not swear, you must go to jail."
> "The will of God be done. For be it known to you, we had rather be in prison and enjoy our peace with God, than be at liberty and break our peace with Him." [12]

Comfort comments that on the income tax return, the oath

and notary are not required, but rather a signature to the
following statement: "I declare under the penalties of per-
jury that this return . . . has been examined by me and to
the best of my knowledge and belief is a true, correct, and
complete return." For the privilege of making that dignified
statement, Quakers in England contended and suffered for
300 years. "What was then a matter of conscience is now a
matter of common sense." [13]

QUAKER HOME LIFE

Two studies throw considerable light on the life of the
Quakers. In 1806, Thomas Clarkson wrote an account of the
Quakers of his day in three volumes entitled *A Portraiture of
Quakerism*. The contemporary picture is provided by Com-
fort in his work, *Quakers in the Modern World*.

According to Clarkson, the Quakers had no particular
interest in art. Normally, there were only three pictures
found in a Quaker home; these were of William Penn's
Treaty with the Indians of the West, a crowded slave ship,
and the plan for the building of Ackworth School near
York. Pictures were used only to exhort people to improve
themselves. The older women wore no ornaments, not even
a plain gold ring in the early days. George Fox deplored
the vanities and fooleries of both men and women of his
day.

> They have lost the adorning of Sarah; they are putting on
> gold and gay apparel; women plaiting the hair, men and
> women powdering it; making their backs look like bags of
> meal . . . they are so lifted up in pride. . . . Likewise the
> women, having their gold, their patches on their faces, noses,
> cheeks, foreheads; having their cuffs double, under the

above, like unto a butcher with his white sleeves; having their ribands tied about their hands, and three or four gold laces about their clothes.[14]

William Penn believed that clothes should be worn only for warmth, for decency, and to distinguish sex.

Since music was associated with worldly people, all instrumental music was banned both in worship and at home. Dancing and dramatics were out of the question. In public libraries under Quaker direction, literature for pleasure was suspect. No prose fiction was permitted, no plays, no novels or "pernicious books." Quakers took an active part in abstinence movements and did not permit the use of alcoholic beverages by members.

The Quakers who believed ardently in social equality refused "hat honor" to all men and women, even refusing to take off their hats before the king. Hats were worn even in the house and were removed only to show honor to someone superior to them: God alone deserved this honor in their eyes. Many Quakers went to jail rather than remove their hats in the court.

Writing from his practical experience of the home life of his community as he has known it for about seventy years, Dr. Comfort reports that though the Quakers appeared to have changed with the times, this change was only in practice, not in spirit. At a wedding or reception in a Quaker home, conversation flows easily, Comfort observes, without the aid of any stimulants. Since many forms of mercantile entertainment have been denied, Quakers have cultivated the pleasures of simple sociability. Over a long period of time, they have been forced to help each other to meet the social demands of the community.

Although the present-day Quakers have comfortable homes, they are never showy and normally not too large. Children are still raised with a respect for manual work and with the skill to perform it efficiently when they grow up. Comfort remarks that this is most helpful in this day when there is a scarcity of domestic help, for the children willingly help with the housework. Simplicity and moderation are primary virtues in a typical Quaker home.

Women today, as in the past, devote much time to their homes and families, but in addition have a number of responsibilities outside their homes. Comfort points out that under the Quaker system, women have always been responsible equals of men and have shared participation with men in the Quaker meetings.

> Their life is perhaps somewhat less distracted than that of some other women, because they do not have to mingle with these good works so many musicales, bridge games, and cocktail parties. As a result, Quaker women enjoy fewer nervous breakdowns, and many live to the advanced age which moderation is alleged to favor.[15]

All musical instruments were banned both in worship and in the home. Comfort reports of a Philadelphia Friend who felt it necessary to confess publicly to the possession of an organ for the entertainment of an invalid daughter. Until the present century, no Quaker educational institution has dared to introduce any musical instrument. Puritanical views of music and dancing have been held among conservative Friends.

Although earlier Quakers refused to have any fiction books, today an exhortation is made by the conservatives to have only wholesome books on the shelves of the library.

While the women in the past wore no ornaments of any kind, today plain gold wedding rings are permitted as a sign of the bond between the married couple. An early twentieth-century Quaker authoress, Amelia M. Gummere, refers to the plain dress of the Quakers in these words: "Their attention to plainness, and to all the details of every-day life, was a natural reaction from dogmatism, royal pre-rogative and worldly extravagance." [16]

Conservative Quakers, including Comfort, deplore the fact that the peace and the serenity of the American home is being threatened by outside forces. Visual teaching aids are frequently considered to reduce instruction to the level of movies. Children are almost ignorant of the Bible. To counteract this supposed break-down in home-life, the Quaker meeting substitutes silence for the maddening noise of the outside world.

EDUCATION OF THE QUAKERS

The early Quakers were concerned with only elementary and practical education. Fox was keenly aware of the need for education and realized the importance of training the children in order to promote the cause of Quakerism. He said:

> Returning towards London by Waltham, I advised the setting up of a school there for teaching boys; and also a women's school to be opened at Shacklewell, for instructing girls and young maidens in whatsoever things were civil and useful in the creation. . . . I would not have any to think that I deny or am against schools for the teaching of children the natural tongues and arts whereby they may do natural things; but all natural tongues and languages

upon the earth make no more than natural men; and the natural man knows not the things of God.[17]

John Bellers (1654–1725), a friend of William Penn, was concerned about the education of the poor and especially with the practical results of education. He said:

Beyond reading and writing, a multitude of scholars is not so useful to the publick as some think; the body requiring more hands and legs to provide for, and support it, than heads to direct it; and if the head grows too big for the body, the whole will fall into the rickets.[18]

Quakers found it difficult in the early days to see the importance of education, since their founder, George Fox, was almost illiterate. Secondly, they felt the Lord could speak to a man's heart better than any human teacher; therefore, they looked to the Inner Light to teach them all they needed to know. In the early days, theological training was discounted by the Quakers. Fox was afraid that with too much theological education a person was more likely to become an old-style Puritan than a Quaker. Quakers were strongly of the opinion that the masses should be educated and, in the early days, the principle emphasis was on religious instruction. The first two schools were established in 1667 in Waltham and Shacklewell; both were for boys. Fox mentions in the *Journal* that children were to be encouraged to learn "whatsoever things were civil and useful in the creation." [19]

Education was given free to the children of poor members; "The master was to be one well skilled in Latin, writing, and arithmetic." [20] Children were to be discouraged from attending schools where they could learn corrupt ways, fashions, and languages of the world. These, Fox felt, would spoil and alienate the minds of children, leading them into averseness or opposition to the truth. In his epistles of 1690, Fox admonished the provision of schoolmasters who were faithful Friends. The lack of regular schools was met by arranging for instruction by qualified members within the Meeting House. Well-known ministers, such as William Edmundson, George Whitehead, and George Keith, took part in such instructions.[21]

The early Quakers believed that education should be practical and should help the recipient gain an honest livelihood. Youth were to be prepared morally to cope with the business of living in this world. The education of poor children was in industrial skills after which suitable positions were found for them. Regular apprenticeship contracts were drawn for the students at the meetings.

This Quaker program had distinct advantages over the haphazard programs of other societies. By receiving adequate wages during the apprenticeship period, the young student was less tempted to abandon his education before completing it. Parents were exhorted in the newly established colonies to provide adequate education for their children. Threatened by a five-pound penalty, parents were enjoined to make sure that their children, at the end of twelve years, were able to read the Bible and to write. After this, they were to teach them some useful trade.[22] This was done so "that none may be idle, but the poor may work to live, and the rich, if they become poor, may not want." [23]

Children were not pampered. Penn, who gave an exemplary education to his children, upheld the following principles:

> Children can't be too hardly bred: For beside that it fits them to bear the Roughest Providences, it is more Masculine,

> Active, and Healthy. Nay, 'tis certain, that the Liberty of
> the Mind is mightly preserved by it. . . . The memory of
> the Ancients is hardly in any Thing more to be celebrated,
> than in a Strict and Useful Institution of the Youth. By
> Labour they prevented Luxury in their young people, till
> wisdom and Philosophy had taught them to resist and
> despise it.[24]

August Jorns, author of *The Quakers as Pioneers in Social
Work,* mentions that the pedagogical results in Ackworth
were altogether good. It has been deduced that the very
great falling off in poverty among the Quakers in the nineteenth century was in a large measure due to this school.[25]

The efforts of the Quakers were primarily directed to the
improvement of their own children. Others were permitted
to join these institutions but education was organized with
the Quaker children in mind. Three types of schools were
set up: Sunday schools primarily for children, especially those
who worked in factories, where instruction was primarily of
a religious nature; and the adult school, where arithmetic
was taught along with the Bible and which was open to anyone, irrespective of denominational allegiance. The Lancaster
schools were the third and most unusual type of school.
Joseph Lancaster, who was born in 1778, started an in-
expensive children's school in which each class had a monitor
who was responsible for the behavior of the class. Lancaster's principle was to keep as silent as possible and let
the students learn by keeping themselves constantly occupied.
If the teacher spelled a word, the students did not merely
listen to the teacher but wrote it down. By a system of
awards, however small, he stimulated their interest.

In time, Quakers opened not only schools, but several

colleges in which the subjects taught were the same as those in non-Quaker institutions. "Handicrafts represent the Quaker belief in some practical skill, and the natural sciences are popular because they reveal the divine handiwork. It is not the curriculum which attracts non-Quakers [to these schools] . . . rather it is the solicitude of the school for the welfare of the individual." [26]

LITERATURE OF THE QUAKERS

The King James Bible was read by most of the merchants, as well as Bibles in other languages. Quakers had been diligent record keepers, not only in the field of business, but also on the history of their "sufferings." Most of the merchants read the *History of the Rise, Increase, and Progress of the Christian People Called Quakers* by the Dutch Quaker, Willem Sewell. Other popular books were the *History of the Rise and Progress of the People Called Quakers in Ireland* by Dr. John Rutty written in 1751, the *Collection of the People Called Quakers* by John Besse, and the dramatic *Journal* of George Fox.

Books on Catholicism such as Fox's *Arraignment of Popery* contained views that were very similar to those of Protestants. Frederick Tolles, author of *Meeting House and Counting House,* points out that the more scholarly Quakers perused works of Catholic theologians either to learn from them or to refute them. The *Summa Theologica* of Thomas Aquinas was found in the library of such learned Quakers as James Logan.[27] Calvin's *Institutes* and Luther's *Catechism* were also found in Logan's library. Books on mystical writings were frequently found in Quaker collections, in-

cluding Anthony Benezet's *Spirit of Prayer* and Thomas
Hartley's *Discourse on Mistakes Concerning Religion, Enthusiasm, Experiences.*

Some Quaker merchants were interested in philosophical
speculation. James Logan, for example, possessed complete
editions of Aristotle in both Greek and Latin including the
Nicomachean Ethics, the *Politics,* and the *History of Animals.* He also possessed Plutarch's *Morals.*

Most Quaker libraries also contained such practical books
as *A Present for an Apprentice,* the subtitle of which was
A Sure Guide to Gain Both Esteem and Estate; the *Essay
upon the Probable Means of Making People Gainers in the
Ballance of Trade,* which although it "accepted the basic
premises of mercantilism, nevertheless argued for relative
freedom of trade"; and John Locke's *Papers Relating to
Money, Interest and Trade.*

Books and periodicals such as the *Tatler, Spectator,
Guardian, Gentleman's Magazine, London Magazine,* Samuel
Johnson's *Rambler* and *Idler* were read by many Quakers.
"Their interests carried most of them far beyond this level
of reading, and gave a few of them title to be mentioned in
the same breath with Virginia gentlemen, Charleston planter-
aristocrats, or Boston merchants and lawyers among the best-
read and most cultivated men in colonial America." [28]

THE QUAKERS AND SOCIAL PROBLEMS

Quakers have never followed a policy of isolation, and have
always been deeply concerned with their neighbors. "Social
order" is the technical term which Quakers employ to designate the living and working conditions prevailing in the com-

munities where they dwell.[29] As August Jorns states, in whatever was undertaken by the Quakers, the attempt was made to create "humane and dignified conditions of living," even for the man who had no property, "as the first prerequisite of morality and religious life." [30] From the beginning of the movement the Quakers have been active in poor relief, education of youth and adults, helping alcoholics, public health, care of the insane, instituting reforms in the prisons, and the abolition of slave trade and slavery.

Poor Relief

Thorold Rogers, author of *Economic Interpretation of History,* says: "The Seventeenth century fastened pauperism on the English labourer, and this is his only inheritance in the strife of that time." [31] The aim of the Quakers was to ameliorate poverty. George Fox long ago exhorted them to take care of the poor, the blind, the lame, the crippled "so that no beggar may be found on English soil, so that you can claim to be the equal of Jews; for they had Law, which provided for widows, orphans, and strangers. Whoever closes his ear to the poor, closes it to the Law." Many petitions were made by Fox to the Parliament, such as the one *To the Protector and Parliament of England* (London, 1658). Thomas Lawson entitled his: *An Appeal to the Parliament, concerning the Poor, that there may not be a Beggar in England* (London, 1660).

Among the practical means employed to achieve their objectives were systematic organization of charity to replace unregulated alms-giving and a leveling of social inequalities to relieve the crushing distress of the lower classes which stood in sharp contrast to the senseless luxury of the upper strata of society. Although a sense of duty could be awakened, "a quicker way would be the prohibition of all frivolous amusement and of unreasonable extravagance in clothing." [32] The early Quaker philosophy was to clothe the naked and feed the hungry from what was left over.

For their part, members of the Quaker community rarely had to resort to public support for their survival. Dr. J. C. Lettsome, author of *Memoirs of John Fothergill, M.D.*, remarked:

> The time may come when a wise legislator may descend to inquire, by what medium a whole society, in both the old and the new world, is made to think and act with uniformity for upwards of a century;—by what polity, without emolument from Government, they have become the only people on earth free from poverty;—by what economy they have thus prevented beggary and want among any of their members, whilst the nation groans under taxes for the poor. [33]

Through the inauguration of monthly meetings especially for the poor, help was organized for poor relief. The principle was instituted that not charity but self-help as far as possible was to be encouraged. Jorns says:

> It was taken as a self-evident principle that everyone should endeavor to support himself through his own work . . . the circumstances of all those who had asked the monthly meeting for help were publicly discussed in the monthly meeting. . . . Only in cases having to do with the support of the dependents of travelling preachers was publicity avoided: the fact that the activity of the breadwinner was for the common good removed the odium from his need of public support. [34]

In addition to the care of the poor, coal was provided if needed; likewise, some help was offered to those in need of medical help. Non-Quakers also received help freely, as may be seen from one of the entries; "Paid to John Haddon for Edward Hall, a person in need, and the widow Cane, a poor old woman, 16 s.," or "Paid to J. Hill for the widow Massey, who is sick and almost blind, 5 s." [35] Help was given the poor through legacies and gifts left to them by wealthy members of the community. Capital sums came into the possession of the Society as early as 1665, 1670, 1672, and 1683.[36]

Unlike the Roman Catholics and some other groups in England, the idea that the poor were necessary for reaping some benefit from the Almighty through alms was totally unacceptable to the Quakers. There was no virtue in increasing the number of the poor; men were encouraged to improve their economic status. Any emigration to America that did not appear to have compelling reasons in its favor, was discouraged. No one was encouraged to emigrate unless there was a distinct possibility of securing employment. However, those who emigrated because of their faith were given monetary help.[37]

Quakers often found it difficult to obtain employment because only certain types of work were permitted by the Society. Since they frowned upon luxury—even those who were prosperous were not permitted to indulge in it—maintaining large numbers of servants was regarded as taboo. This type of work was considered unproductive. If a Quaker needed work urgently, he was permitted to work as a servant in a Quaker household, but this was only as a temporary measure until suitable productive work was obtainable. During the entire period, he was under the supervision of the meetings.

John Bellars (1654–1725), wrote the *Proposals for Raising a Colledge of Industry, etc.,* which had three objectives for the workers:

First, profit for the rich (which is life for the rest). Secondly, a plentiful living for the poor, without difficulty.
Thirdly, a good education for youth, that may tend to
prepare their souls into the nature of good ground. . . .
However prevalent arguments of charity may be to some,
when profit is joined with it, it will raise most money,
provide for most people, hold longest, and do most good:
for what sap is to a tree, that profit is to all business, by
increasing and keeping it alive.[38]

Bellars' rationally calculated plan was to settle 300 workers
in a colony; 200 would support the community while the
remaining 100 would work for the pure profit of those who
advanced the capital.

Quaker society became more homogeneous as time went
by. Though it did not exclusively consist of well-to-do persons, a majority of the members were middle class. The
original comfortable farmers and artisans were gradually
replaced by merchants, who sometimes achieved the status
of capitalists and bankers. "The Quakers made out best as
merchants and bankers, since through their absolute reliabil-
ity they won the confidence of the public. The introduction
of the one-price system of selling is credited to them." [39]

The yearly meetings confirmed the members in the virtues
of simplicity because the rich man was only a steward of the
wealth entrusted to him by the Lord. Welfare plans for the
needy were extended to cover those employed by the Quaker
employers. Thomas Carlyle regarded a Quaker as an ideal
employer.[40] At the beginning of the century, the Cadbury
family in England founded a model colony for their employees at Bournville. Similarly, Fry and Rowntree, chocolate
makers, followed the example of a typical Quaker employer
and instituted a welfare program for their employees. Today

non-Quaker employers have been moved by the Quaker example and have instituted commendable welfare programs for their employees.

Spirituous Liquors

The Quakers were not opposed to alcoholic beverages if moderation was practiced. At the workhouse in Clerkenwell, established in 1702, "sufficient beer" was permitted as part of the ration. Beer and wine were served at the business meetings (these drinks, however, have now been replaced by coffee or tea).[41] This is not surprising as in the early days of Quakerism, alcoholic beverages were considered not only to be harmless, but also to have food value.

During the reign of Charles II, wine and brandy were often imported from France. However, the increasing use of alcohol proved to be detrimental to the public health and morals, and finally produced negative economic effects. Later, in their yearly meetings, Quakers began to urge the faithful to curtail the use of alcohol. The government set up an import tariff on alcohol to curb its misuse in England.

William Penn in Pennsylvania took a dim view of the use of alcohol and forbade its use as far as possible. He said: "To wink at a trade that effeminates the people, and invades the ancient discipline of the kingdom, is a crime capital, and to be severely punished instead of being excused by the magistrate." [42] He deplored the use of alcohol as a means of outwitting the Indians by making them drunk and taking undue advantage of them. Similarly, in England the Quakers exhorted the members as well as nonmembers against the evils of alcohol by preaching about the sad consequences of excessive drunkenness. George Whitehead, a member of Par-

liament, who in 1695 led the first successful Quaker effort
for relief from the oath of allegiance to the Church of England required by Parliament, writes:

> You who keep alehouses, take thought in the fear of God
> . . . perform your office so as to keep your consciences clear
> in the sight of God and man. Do not make your living from
> the sins of the people; do not let your profits from this
> source. Be careful not to offer to any man or woman more
> strong liqueur than is necessary to their refreshment and
> their health.[43]

By 1778, the Quakers were convinced that manufacturing
of liquor was sinful because the grains used for distilling and
beer-making increased the price of bread and, therefore, hurt
the poor. Bread was for sustenance and not to be converted
into anything that would destroy human life. Alcohol was
barred from all social gatherings, private and public. Temperance societies appeared in America and England, especially
when in 1826 two-thirds of the pauperism, nine-tenths of the
crime, and two-thirds of all cases of mental disease were
traced (rightly or wrongly) to the use of alcohol.[44] In 1839,
it was decided that not moderation but total abstinence be
recommended to the members, thus abolishing beer as well
as wine. The Quakers brought their influence to bear upon
their members to practice total abstinence, and also persuaded
members of society at large to curtail its use as far as possible.
Protests were lodged with officials to forbid the sale of liquor
to the prisoners in Pennsylvania. A report of the Friends'
Temperance Association of 1945 deplored the fact that while
teachers in thousands of rural schools earn less than five
hundred dollars a year, a million Negro children had been
without any schooling at all. Meanwhile, thousands of houses

remain unfit for human habitation. At the same time, Americans spend several billion dollars annually for a product (liquor) that improves neither one's ability or efficiency and makes no one a healthier person, a finer person, a finer Christian, or a more useful citizen.[45]

Health Problems

Quakers were not only concerned with the health problems of their immediate members but also with those of the community at large. With the migration of the rural population to the industrial areas, the established charitable help of the churches was no longer available. In 1714, John Bellars wrote an *Essay Towards the Improvement of Physick in Twelve Proposals* which was "dedicated to the Parliament of Great Britain." He was the first person to advocate the establishment of hospitals for the poor. "The dead are to be dissected for the instruction of the physicians." [46] Bellars proposed that separate hospitals be established for specific kinds of diseases; the blind would be treated separately. One hospital was planned exclusively for the purposes of study and experiment "that full knowledge may be gained such as may prevent the Queen, in case she should fall ill, from receiving the wrong kind of treatment." [47]

Bellars was concerned by the premature death of productive laborers. Education was a public duty because it made a man a productive worker. Similarly, he must be kept in good health for the very important reason that the community would then reap full benefit through his person. By Bellars' calculation, the premature death of a productive laborer was a loss of about £200 annually. He invited the wealthy to make their own estimate in their own particular case.

The Quaker physician, John Fothergill, pleaded for sanitary conditions in the city of London and attempted to secure the official registration of births and deaths.[48] His investigations into the relation between sickness and weather conditions were published.

The insane were not regarded as often curable, as they are at present. As late as 1770, Bedlam Asylum in London permitted the insane to be exhibited openly to the public as entertainment, which brought in a considerable amount of income. The Quakers pleaded for humane treatment for the insane, the abolition of chains, and the rigid separation of the sexes. William Tuke in York called a meeting of the members "for the purpose of taking into consideration the property of providing a retired habitation, with necessary advice . . . for members of our Society and others in profession with us, who may be in a state of lunacy or so deranged in mind as to require such provision." [49] Visitors from all over the world came to see the model institution.

In America, deaf-mute girls were persecuted as if cursed. The Quaker, Anthony Benezet, interested himself in their plight and gave them instruction.[50] Thus, through the influence of the Quakers, the insane and deaf, instead of being regarded as demon-possessed, were increasingly looked upon as merely sick, and thus capable of rehabilitation.

Prison Reform

Quakers also had a vital interest in prison reform movements. This was natural since many of the members had been "guests" of the government and were acquainted with the miserable conditions found within the prison walls. They did not bribe their jailers and, therefore, could expect no relief from the misery of the jails.

Quakers agitated for a thorough reform of the prisons. The prisons were dungeon-like and often consisted of underground rooms. Overcrowding was a rule; filth and dirt were common. There was little classification and prisoners of all classes were thrown together. The sexes were not segregated. Prisoners had to supply their own food. Since jailers were poorly paid, they often resorted to trafficking in food and drink for the prisoners. "The management of a prison was not considered a fit occupation for a decent person . . . there was no sort of occupation to divert the attention of the inmates, even for a short interval—the prisons were thus breeding places of crime." [51] According to Quaker philosophy, reform, not punishment, should be the aim of imprisonment. The existing laws imposed the death penalty for over one hundred different crimes. There was no sense of justice whatever; no distinction between major and minor crime existed. It was through Fox's influence that in 1653 the death penalty was abolished for all crimes with the exception of murder. Visitors to the prison were entertained regularly by the open flogging of women inmates. Executions were also a source of entertainment for the masses. John Bellars was concerned not only with the actual betterment of the prisoners, but also with the prevention of crime itself. While Fox believed the death penalty should be used sparingly, Bellars wrote about the desirability of abolishing the death penalty altogether.

John Howard, probably the foremost prison reformer of his day, was summoned by the House of Commons to testify on the conditions in prison. Largely through his efforts, jailers for the first time received a fixed salary, sanitary conditions were improved, and the prisons were made more fit for human habitation. Elizabeth Fry and her associates helped to improve the appalling lot of women prisoners. Many of the mothers in the prisons had their children with them because they had been born there. The children were naked and under-nourished. Through Howard's influence, separate confinement of prisoners was instituted to overcome the filth and vice that resulted from the indiscriminate herding in most of the jails.

In keeping with the Quaker philosophy that the convicted criminal has certain rights and the regeneration of the prisoner is of utmost importance, a new type of prison was instituted—the Pennsylvania Prison. Regeneration was to be achieved by allowing the prisoner to have plenty of time to reflect upon his evil ways, and permit the Inner Light to do the work of reformation within the man. The word penitentiary came to be used in this connection.

In the New Wymondham jail in England, separation of hardened from first and petty offenders and of men from women was introduced, as well as separate cells at night, work in shops during the day, and solitary confinement of the most incorrigible offenders. In certain cases the inmate never worked with anyone else but remained in his cell, being taken out only for a little exercise in the yard. Under these circumstances he had plenty of time for reflection and opportunity for reformation. The principal idea of the Pennsylvania cellular isolation was to separate the inmate from all other bad elements in the prison so that he would not be corrupted any further. Howard, it seems, borrowed this idea from the Hospice of Saint Michael which used cellular isolation in order to reform delinquent boys. According to Thorsten Sellin, this concept of cellular isolation dates back to the practice of contemplation in monastery cells and to monastic rule.⁵² Eventually its modification, the Auburn system, triumphed. Here the prisoner was confined as much as possible, but was permitted to congregate while working during the day. Howard's idea that the inmate is not to be punished but reformed, and that prevention is better than cure has continued to influence prison reformers.

Race Relations

When the Quakers arrived in America they were confronted by two races they had not met before: the American Indians and the Negroes. From the beginning, they decided to give precedence to the Christian viewpoint rather than the more expedient one which suggested that economic exploitation at any cost was desirable. They befriended the Indians in Pennsylvania and received, in turn, friendship unknown to most other colonists. William Penn succeeded in making treaties with the Indians and wrote that the Indians "believe in God and immortality, without the help of metaphysics." This was particularly pleasing to the Quakers and throughout the years of Quaker control of Pennsylvania, from 1682 until 1756, the relations between the Quakers and the Indians were most cordial.

George Fox had visited Barbados and met Negroes and some of the Quakers banished to Jamaica had become acquainted with Negroes. The Quakers believed that Christ had died for all men—including the Indians and the Negroes—and that each had an eternal soul in spite of his different skin color. The Quakers at first were interested in impressing upon the Negroes their Christian obligations to their masters and to each other. They discouraged violence, drunkenness, polygamy, and other vices.⁵³ But the inhuman treatment of the

Negroes finally compelled the Quakers to change their ideas and to recognize the total incompatibility of slaveholding with the Christian point of view which they held. After much study, private investigation, and thought, they waged a battle against the practice of slavery, formed antislavery societies and, in 1784, distributed innumerable pamphlets. The slave traders promptly issued denunciations of the antislavery propaganda. The Quakers proceeded to petition the federal government and in 1794 an act prohibiting the export of slaves was passed. In 1799, the regulations governing slave transportation were made materially more exacting. After the turn of the century, the question was finally settled in favor of the oppressed race.[54]

The efforts of the Quakers in behalf of the oppressed races are still being carried on. In 1945, at the time of the Japanese evacuation, the Quakers set up temporary hostels, provided clothing, and cared for the infirm. The present views of the Quakers may best be summarized in the words of the Report of the Committee on Race Relations of the Yearly Meeting:

> We must secure for every man, regardless of race, creed or color, the right to earn a living for himself and for those he loves. This right is almost as sacred as the right to life itself. Every child must have the right to grow up in an environment in which he has decent chance to develop as a healthy and normal human being. Because of the use of restrictive covenants and other racial caste pressures the great majority of the Negroes are denied the basic right. . . . Only one issue is involved, the fundamental equality of all men in the sight of God.[55]

War and Peace

Pacificism has always been closely associated with Quakerism. Although most people are interested in peace, the Quakers have sought peace in a positive manner over the last three hundred years. When George Fox asserted that he would not engage in fighting at any time, he looked to the Apostle James to support his position. Fox said: "I knew from whence all wars arose, even from the lust, according to James' doctrine; and that I lived in the virtue of that life and power that took away the occasion of all wars." In one of his letters Fox states:

> The devil is the author and cause of all wars and strife, all that pretend to fight for Christ are deceived; for His kingdom is not of this world. Therefore, His servants do not fight. Fighters are not of Christ's kingdom, but are without Christ's kingdom. . . . Live in love and peace with all men, keep out of all the bustlings of the world; meddle not with the powers of the earth; but mind the kingdom, the way of peace.[56]

The Quakers carried Fox's ideas to the New World. Instead of fighting with the Indians, they made friends with them, and bought land from them at a price agreeable to the Indians rather than confiscating it.

It has not always been easy to maintain a position of pacifism. When one's country is threatened by an aggressor, it is very difficult not to take up arms in its defense. Charles M. Woodman says that over the years there have developed at least three different courses of action on the part of the Society toward those who felt they could not follow the pacifist program. At first when a young person knowingly left the Quaker group and entered into conflict, the Quakers naturally did not feel responsible for his spiritual welfare. Henceforth, the young man understood that he had no right to receive any spiritual guidance from any of the Quaker groups. Second, during the quietistic period when military service was considered an offense, the meetings, in many instances, dismissed the young soldiers from the membership. However, over the course of the years the emphasis has given way to a growing Quaker concern with saving the individual's spiritual experience and guarding human conscience. During the last two world wars, the Society made a determined effort to keep in sympathetic touch with the members wherever they scattered in the world.[57]

Quakers inevitably were regarded as "spies" and "traitors" because of their refusal to come to the aid of their country during the Mexican and Civil wars. They felt that a positive stand against war was better than taking up arms and paying a high cost in physical suffering and human losses. Their early experiences with the Indians reinforced their notions of pacificism. Although the Quakers suffered for their beliefs, they eventually persuaded the government that there is an adequate place for conscience to function within the law.

During World War I they "made the proposition that the conscientious objector to war should be released to go into the war-stricken areas and render all the aid possible." [58] This request was granted and the American Friends Service Committee was organized which distributed food and other supplies in all the countries of the world. Many a youth during the First World War was exempted from the armed forces to work in an agricultural activity. An exemption paragraph in the Selective Service Act of 1948, which was approved by the Quakers, reads:

Nothing contained in this title shall be construed to require any person to be subject to combatant training and service in the armed forces of the United States who, by reason of religious training and belief, is conscientiously opposed to participation in war in any form. Religious training and belief in this connection means an individual's belief in a relation to a Supreme Being involving duties superior to those arising from any human relation, but does not include essentially political, sociological, or philosophical views or a merely personal moral code. Any person claiming exemption from combatant training and service because of such conscientious objections whose claim is sustained by the local board shall, if he is inducted into the armed forces under this title, be assigned to non-combatant service as defined by the President, or shall if he is found to be conscientiously opposed to participation in such noncombatant service, be deferred.

The Quakers have never compromised on the issue of war and peace. Promoting world peace has been their unfailing objective. There is a regular Peace Committee that works ceaselessly toward this end. During World War II many Quaker young men went to prison for their conscience' sake. A letter to such members reads in part as follows:

Third Month 30, 1945

Dear Friend:

We wish to express our love and concern for thee as one of our members who are imprisoned for conscience' sake. Though we have missed thee in person, we know that the strength of thy spirit has been with us. . . . It is with deep humility that we realize how few of us are making any sacrifice or testimony for the way of love and peace among men. May thy courage and steadfastness of purpose be an example to us who find too many excuses and reasons for not seeking out and following the Light. We are, with love, thy friends.[59]

Rufus Jones interprets pacifism as "peace making." The pacifist is literally a peace maker. He is not a passive or negative person who proposes to lie back and do nothing in the face of injustice, unrighteousness, and rampant evil. "Pacifism is not a theory; it is a way of life. It is something you are and do." [60]

SUMMARY

The everyday ethic of Quakerism is dominated by the principles that all men are equal and that all men can come immediately into the presence of God, needing no human being to represent them before their Father who is in heaven. In his worship, the Quaker seeks to cultivate the divine aspect of life. The Inner Light directs his life within and without. He stresses utmost simplicity in his clothing, his motto being that clothing is for decency and not for pride. Language is regulated so as not to offend superiors and, simultaneously, not to forget that all men are equal. Hence, the use of "thee" and "thou." All trivial words are omitted; no oaths or swearing are permitted.

Quaker home life is devoid of all worldly amusements such as music, plays, novels, and "pernicious books." Alcoholic beverages are forbidden. In the early days, education was not considered vital but, gradually, its importance came to be realized. Presently there are many Quaker educational institutions organized throughout the world.

The Quakers have increasingly attempted to improve living and working conditions throughout the community. Not charity, but self-help, is encouraged. Welfare plans for the needy have been instituted wherever possible. Outstanding contributions have been made in the establishment of hospitals, prison reforms, and in the care of the blind, deaf, and insane. Improving race relations, especially with the American Indian and the Negro, has also been stressed.

With the Quakers, pacifism is a way of life. For the last three hundred years, most Quakers have preferred to suffer rather than to take up arms.

NOTES

1. Charles M. Woodman, *Quakers Find a Way* (Indianapolis, 1950), p. 35.
2. I John 1:6.
3. I John 2:27.
4. Howard Brinton, *Friends For 300 Years* (New York, 1952), p. 59.
5. Woodman, *Quakers Find a Way,* p. 48.
6. Charles Lamb, "A Quakers' Meeting" as cited in Woodman, *Quakers Find a Way,* pp. 52–53.
7. Woodman, *Quakers Find a Way,* p. 66.
8. William Penn, *Some Fruits of Solitude* (London, 1915), passim.
9. Woodman, *Quakers Find a Way,* p. 44.
10. Ibid., p. 54.
11. William Wistar Comfort, *Quakers in the Modern World* (New York, 1949), p. 132.
12. Ibid., p. 134.
13. Ibid., p. 138.
14. Ibid., p. 127.
15. Ibid., p. 121.

16. Amelia M. Gummere, *The Quaker: A Study in Costume* (Philadelphia, 1901), passim.

17. George Fox, *Gospel Truth Demonstrated* (London, 1706), p. 653.

18. John S. Bellers, *Proposals of Raising a Colledge of Industry of all Useful Trades and Husbandry, With Profit for the Rich, A Plentiful Living For the Poor, and a Good Education for the Youth* (London, 1696), p. 17.

19. George Fox, *Journal* (New York, 1924), p. 89.

20. W. Beck and T. F. Ball, *The London Friends' Meetings* (London, 1869), p. 131.

21. August Jorns, *The Quakers as Pioneers in Social Work* trans. Thomas Kite Brown (New York, 1931), p. 103.

22. Ibid., p. 109.

23. Isaac Sharpless, *A Quaker Experiment in Government* (Philadelphia, 1898), pp. 35 ff.

24. William Penn, *Some Fruits of Solitude in Reflections and Maxims* (London, 1905), p. 138.

25. Jorns, *Quakers as Pioneers,* p. 115.

26. Comfort, *Quakers in the Modern World,* p. 172.

27. Frederick B. Tolles, *Meeting House and Counting House* (Chapel Hill, N. C., 1948), pp. 163, 164, 167, 204.

28. Ibid.

29. Comfort, *Quaker in Modern World,* p. 175.

30. Jorns, *Quakers as Pioneers,* p. 98.

31. Thorold James Rogers, *Economic Interpretation of History* (New York, 1909), p. 266.

32. Jorns, *Quakers as Pioneers,* p. 57.

33. J. C. Lettsom, *Memoirs of John Fothergill, M.D.* (London, 1786). Quoted in F. M. Eden, *State of the Poor, or a History of the Labouring Classes in England* (London, 1928), passim.

34. Jorns, *Quakers as Pioneers,* p. 62.

35. From *Yearly Meeting, Minutes for 1737,* as cited in Jorns, *Quakers as Pioneers,* p. 65.

36. Ibid, p. 66.

37. Ibid., p. 70.

38. Bellers, *Proposals of Colledge of Industry,* pp. 1–2.

39. Jorns, *Quakers as Pioneers,* p. 87.

40. Thomas Carlyle, *Past and Present,* in *Works,* bk. 4, chap. 5 (London, 1928), p. 343.

41. Jorns, *Quakers as Pioneers,* p. 131.

42. Ibid., p. 135.

43. Ibid., p. 136.

44. Ibid., p. 140.

45. *Proceedings of the Yearly Meeting of the Religious Society of Friends of Philadelphia and Vicinity* (Philadelphia, 1945), p. 209.

46. Jorns, *Quakers as Pioneers,* p. 147.

47. Ibid.

48. Ibid., p. 149.

49. Samuel Tuke, *Description of the Retreat* (London, 1813), p. 20.

50. Jorns, *Quakers as Pioneers,* p. 158.

51. Ibid., p. 165.

52. Harry Elmer Barnes, "The Historical Origin of the Prison System in America," *Journal of Criminal Law and Criminology* 12 (1920–1921):42–43.

Thorsten Sellin, "Don Jean Mabilon—A Prison Reformer of the Seventeenth Century," *Journal of Criminal Law and Criminology* 17 (1926–1927):601–602.

53. Jorns, *Quakers as Pioneers,* p. 201.

54. Ibid., p. 222.

55. *Proceedings of the Yearly Meeting . . . of Philadelphia and Vicinity,* p. 200.

56. Margaret E. Hirst, *The Quakers in Peace and War* (New York, 1923), p. 60.

57. Woodman, *Quakers Find a Way,* p. 242.

58. Ibid.

59. *Proceedings of the Yearly Meeting . . . of Philadelphia and Vicinity,* p. 144.

60. Rufus Jones, *The New Quest* (New York, 1928), p. 97.

4

ECONOMIC ETHIC OF QUAKERS

In the early period of the movement, Quakers faced considerable hostility from public officials. In England, they were persecuted by the established church and the king. Because of their refusal to take oaths, their resistance to the imposition of tithes, and their insistence on freedom of worship, they were imprisoned, their meetings broken up, and their property seized or destroyed. Despite this hostility, the early Quakers flourished. They were barred from government service, the learned professions, and the universities. Their pacifism prohibited service in the army or navy. Trade and industry were among the few economic areas open to them. Through energy, honesty, and native ability they became prosperous and achieved a degree of influence far beyond what might have been expected from a small, persecuted group.

They are responsible for uniform pricing. Their one-price system, without discrimination, won the confidence of the public and brought Quaker tradesmen a large portion of the trade. They became leaders in iron manufacturing. A Quaker devised the smelting of iron ore by coal instead of wood—a development important in the expansion of the industry. Increasing use of iron in armaments, however, brought an end to Quaker dominance in the industry. This removal was voluntary on the part of the Quaker manufacturers. Quakers built the first iron bridge and financed the first railways. They were also active in copper and lead mining and brass manufacturing.

Their industrial activities extended to weaving and textile manufacturing, shipping, pottery making, pharmaceutical manufacturing, the manufacture of scientific instruments, and clock-making. Their widespread reputation for probity led many people to deposit their savings with Quakers at a time when banks were virtually nonexistent. Along with the increasing need for banking facilities in their own operations, public confidence brought Quakers into the banking business. The history of Barclay's, Lloyd's, and other great banking institutions, illustrates Quaker enterprise. A contemporary example of Quaker business operations is the English chocolate and cocoa industry dominated by the well known names of Cadbury, Fry, and Rowntree. In spite of all the opposition once directed against them, this minority group succeeded in commercial undertakings.

THE WAY TO WEALTH

Contemporaries are familiar with many "How To" books: *Think and Grow Rich, The Law of Success, How to Accumulate Wealth,* etc. William Penn wrote such a book on the economic virtues for the benefit of the Quakers: *The Advice of William Penn to His Children*. A passage often quoted reads:

> Diligence is (a) Virtue useful and laudable among Men: It is a discreet and understanding Application of one's Self to Business; and avoids the extremes of Idleness and Drudgery. It gives great advantages to Men: It loses not Time, it conquers Difficulties, recovers Disappointments, gives Dispatch, Supplies Want of Parts; and is that to them, which a Pond is to Spring; tho' it has no Water of itself, it will keep what it gets, and is never dry. . . . Shun Diversions, think only of the present Business, till that be done. . . . Diligence (for Solomon) is the Way to Wealth: The diligent hand makes rich (Proverbs 10:4). . . . It prefers Men. . . . Seest thou a Man diligent in his Business he shall stand before Kings. (Proverbs 22:29). It preserves an Estate. . . . There is no living upon the Principal, you must be diligent to preserve what you have, whether it be Acquisition or Inheritance; else it will consume.
> Frugality is a Virtue too, and not of little Use in Life, the better Way to be Rich, for it has less Toil and Temptation. It is proverbial. A Penny sav'd is a Penny got; It has a significant Moral; for this Way of getting is more in your own Power and less subject to Hazard, as well as Snares, free of Envy, void of Suits, and is beforehand with Calamities. For many get that cannot keep, and for Want of Frugality spend what they get and so come to want what they have spent.[1]

Though Ben Franklin was not a Quaker, he was nevertheless influenced by the same Puritan background as were the Quakers. This probably accounts for the similarity in the ideas of Franklin and those of the Quakers as may be observed when the above passage is compared with some of Franklin's formulations.

THE QUAKER MERCHANTS

The Quakers did not have an easy time in the world of business, for during the early days of Quakerism, businessmen did not have the prestige they enjoy today. Concerning Quaker acquisitive talents, Giovanni Paolo Marana at the turn of the nineteenth century wrote:

> As to these modern Seducers, they are not Men of *Arms* but a herd of silly insignificant People, aiming rather to heap up Riches in Obscurity, than to acquire a Fame by an heroick Undertaking. They are generally Merchants and Mechanicks, and are observ'd to be very punctual in their Dealings, Men of few Words in a Bargain, modest and compos'd in their Deportment, temperate in their Lives and using great Frugality in all Things. In a Word, they are singularly Industrious, sparing no Labour or Pains to increase their Wealth; and so subtle and inventive, that they would, if possible, extract Gold out of Ashes. I know none that excel them in these Characters but the *Jews* and the *Banians:* The former being the craftiest of all Men, and the latter so superlatively cunning that they will over-reach the Devil.[2]

Banking institutions were established at a very early date in Philadelphia. Since some of the strongest colonial merchants and mercantile firms had their offices there, banking institutions were necessary. William Edmundson, who was at all times more concerned with the spiritual than the material welfare of the Friends, was led to exclaim: "Such a Spirit came in amongst us, as was amongst the *Jews,* when they came up out of Egypt, this began to look back into the World, and *traded* with the *Credit* which was not of it's own purchasing, striving to be great in the Riches and Possessions of this World." [3] In Philadelphia, the Quakers were very sound financiers and businessmen. One critic remarked: "The Quakers are a People that mistake their Interest as seldom as any, being Men of Industry, and Experience, such as are intent upon their Business, Cunning in their Bargains, and Crafty upon all occasions for their own ends. . . . These *Children of Light* have been so much Wiser than the *Children of this World,* that 'tis now good Advice to look to your Pockets when you have any dealings with the Quakers." [4]

In the taverns, around 1744, Presbyterians, Anglicans, Roman Catholics, Methodists, Moravians, and Anabaptists were engrossed in such important topics as politics and religion, while the Quakers "talked only about selling of flour and the low price it bore." [5] The export business of the Quakers increased to such an extent that a merchant in New York remarked: "The Quakers and the Jews are the men nowadays." [6] Of the wealthiest seventeen persons in Philadelphia in 1764, eight professed membership in the Quaker sect, four had been reared in the Quaker faith, five were non-Quakers, and one—William Shippen—owed the basis of his fortune to his Quaker grandfather. [7]

THE SECRET OF QUAKER SUCCESS

While the Quakers arrived on the scene at Philadelphia at an early date and, therefore, could claim a consequent economic advantage over all subsequent rivals, Tolles is eager to point out that this is hardly an adequate explanation for the overwhelming preeminence of the Quakers in Philadelphia. Furthermore, it is wholly inapplicable to the situation of the Quakers in England who achieved comparable economic success in spite of their persecution, and at a strong initial disadvantage in relation to the businessmen of other religious persuasion.[8]

Both in America and in England the Quakers constituted a peculiar religious minority. Persons as different as Voltaire and Sombart have advanced arguments that because the Quakers were excluded by statute or conscientious scruple from government office and from all the professions except medicine, their best talents were utilized in trade and commerce.[9] While this interpretation is not without considerable validity and could be applied to the English Quakers, it is subject to a number of qualifications when applied to the Quakers of Pennsylvania.[10] It is certainly true that the refusal of the Quakers to take oaths barred them from active participation in English political life, but the reason the Quakers did not enter the universities and qualify themselves for a professional life was not because of the barrier or the matriculation oath required of every university entrant, but rather because of their general distrust of the universities. In the eyes of the Quakers, the influence of the universities was most undesirable. They did not enter law for they found it odious to the extent that led Fox to remark: "Away with those lawyers, twenty shillings Councellors, thirty shilling Sergents, ten groat Attourneys, that will throw men into Prison for a thing of nought." [11]

Because of their pacifism, the Quakers could not enter the armed forces or the navy. Rather than remain in the rural areas, the Quakers migrated to the cities. In 1806, Thomas Clarkson reported that "Quakers were flocking into the towns, and abandoning agricultural pursuits." Clarkson believed that this Quaker migration was due to their objection to the payment of tithes. However, he added that "the large and rapid profits frequently made in trade, compared with the generally small and slow returns from agricultural concerns, may probably have operated with many, as an inducement to such a change." [12] Tolles observes that Clarkson's hypothesis does not apply to the Quakers in Pennsylvania.[13]

The only profession that a Quaker could enter on either side of the Atlantic was medicine. Pennsylvania did not require oaths of allegiance from those seeking to hold office, and important posts in the government were held by Quakers. They also served as justices of the peace and a few became outstanding lawyers. In spite of this freedom in Pennsylvania to enter noncommercial fields, many of the Quakers continued to drift into a commercial life.

THE INFLUENCE
OF THE PROTESTANT ETHIC

The explanation for their unusual economic success, both in England and in America, must be sought in some inherent characteristic of Quakerism, common to Quakers on both sides of the Atlantic. Tolles formulated the inevitable question; "Where shall we find it except in their religious and social philosophy?" [14] Long ago, Weber suggested that an intimate relationship existed between certain of the distinctive characteristics of Protestantism and those of early modern capitalism. Along with Weber and Troeltsch, Tolles feels that they possessed a certain affinity, and as Troeltsch states, "the Calvinistic ethic of the 'calling' and of work, which declares that the earning of money with certain precautions is allowable, was able to give capitalism an intellectual and ethical backbone, and that therefore, thus organized and inwardly supported, it vigorously developed, even though within the limits of anti-mammon." [15]

THE INFLUENCE OF CALVINISM

Richard Schlatter observed that "Puritans who turned Quaker did not shed their puritanism." [16] It is virtually impossible to understand Quakerism without taking into consideration their Puritan background. The Puritans turned to the Bible for their guidance for everyday ethical problems. The Quakers looked to the Inner Light. In doing so, they did not shed Puritanism, but reinforced it. The Inner Light never implied laxity in ethical behavior. Moreover, the Quakers were never so engrossed with the Inner Light that they had no time for the outside world. They wished "to be in the world and yet not be of it."

There was nothing negative or passive about their beliefs. Contemplation was only a prelude to an active participation in the things of the world. In their religious experience, Tolles observes, Fox and his associates had more in common with the Hebrew prophets than with the great mystics of the church. They traveled about England calling men to abandon their sins and the vanities of this world, exhorting them to be faithful to the Inward Light of Christ. "Indeed the early Quakers went beyond their Puritan contemporaries. They were frankly perfectionist in their ethical teaching." [17] The golden rule was to be applied here and now on this earth with the help of the Holy Spirit.

The Quakers identified divine law primarily with the Sermon on the Mount, regarding its ethic of love as literally binding upon all who follow Christ. With this Anabaptist position, however, "they combined the essentially Calvinistic conviction that religion must be integrated with life on the natural plane; in other words, they recognized no cleavage between the spheres of divine and natural law." [18] While they agreed with the high ethical code of the Anabaptists, they rejected their monastic attitude toward the material world. In William Penn's words:

> The Christian Convent and Monastery are within, where the Soul is encloistered from Sin. And this Religious House the True of Christ carry about with them, who exempt not themselves from the conversation of the World, though they keep themselves from the Evil of the World in their Conversation. . . . True Godliness don't turn Men out of the World, but enables them to live better in it, and excites their Endeavours to mend it.[19]

Fox addressed Quaker merchants as follows: "So every one strive to be rich in the life, and in the kingdom and things of the world . . . and let him that buys or sells, or possesses, or uses this world, be as if he did not." [20] Perry Miller refers to this as the doctrine of loving the world with "weaned affections . . . a staple moral of Puritan discourse." [21]

There are always risks encountered in any business venture, and Quakers were not exempt from them. A man's entire philosophy is often revealed when he is confronted with a major loss. In 1748, Israel Pemberton wrote a letter to his father after one of his ships disappeared. Such experiences, he said:

> tend to wean the Mind from delighting in transitories and if rightly improv'd—dispose us to look after Enjoyments

more certain and permanent . . . I am sensible there's Satisfaction and I believe Something of a duty, in doing for ourselves: the Principle of True Religion being Active and
never disposes the Mind to Indolence and Sloth, but it
likewise Leads us to Consider, I may say often reminds us
of the End and Purpose of our Views and Persuits, and
Reproves us for them, if not Consistent with the one Point
to which they ought Solely to tend, the Honour of God
and Good of Mankind.[22]

Tolles asserts that in the Quaker's mind, the "Good of
Mankind" represented a positive claim upon his material
wealth. The prospect of being able to help those in need
operated as an incentive to further acquisition.[23] The concept
of calling was not foreign to Quakers. In one of his Epistles,
Fox said:

Train up your children in the fear of God . . . and as
they are capable, they may be instructed and kept employed
in some lawful calling, that they may be diligent, serving
the Lord in the things that are good; that none may live
idle, and be destroyers of the creation.[24]

All vocations were treated as being equal in value. Even
menial tasks were regarded as being important to the Lord.
William Penn, therefore, could exclaim; "The perfection of
Christian Life extends to every honest Labour or Traffic used
among Men." [25] No special credit was claimed by any Quaker
minister. Quaker historians, including Tolles, are generally
in agreement that Thomas Chalkley (1675–1741), a merchant, sea-captain and Quaker minister, has summed up best
The Quaker rationale of the concept of calling. Chalkley
states:

We have liberty from God, and his dear Son, lawfully, and
for Accommodation's Sake, to work or seek for Food or

Raiment; tho' that ought to be a Work of Indifferency, compar'd to great Work of Salvation. Our Saviour saith, Labour not for the Meat which perisheth, but for that which endureth for ever, or to eternal life: By which we do not understand, that Christians must neglect their necessary Occasions and their outward Trades and Callings; but that their chief Labour, and greatest Concern ought to be for their future Well-being in his glorious Kingdom; else why did our Lord say to his Disciples: Children, have you any Meat? They answered, No; and he bid them cast their Nets into the Sea, and they drew to Land a Net full of great Fishes; and Fishing being their Trade, no doubt but they sold them, for it was not likely they could eat 'em all themselves. . . . By this, and much more, which might be noted, it appears that we not only have Liberty to labour in Moderation, but we are given to understand that it is our Duty so to do. The Farmer, the Tradesman, and the Merchant, do not understand by our Lord's Doctrine, that they must neglect their Calling, or grow idle in their Business, but must certainly work, and be industrious in their Callings.[26]

The Calvinists adhered to the idea of the necessity of proving one's faith through wordly activity. Similarly, the Quakers, by laboring diligently in their chosen calling, expected the Lord to bestow His blessing in the form of material prosperity. The Calvinists observed the hand of the Lord in all things; the Quakers regarded business success as a sign that the Lord was indeed guiding them with the Inward Light. Tolles observes that with God's blessing, the faithful and diligent Friend, living austerely in accordance with the "Simplicity of Truth," almost inevitably accumulated wealth for "the Honour of God and Good of Mankind."

Each Quaker was expected to listen to the Inner Voice,

not only for spiritual guidance, but also for any opportunity to improve trade. James Logan, William Penn's secretary who traded in furs and skins, was not satisfied until every opportunity was exploited. Logan writes: "Should I with open eyes [after entering Indian trade] give away those advantages that by God's Blessing my own Industry and management have . . . thrown on me to others who have had no part in that Management . . . I could never account for it to my Self and family." [27]

The Quakers never set a limit on the amount of material prosperity desirable. Moreover, there was no question of taking it easy. The virtues of industry and frugality were held in high repute among Quakers, while idleness was considered as a root of vice. Even while in prison, William Penn discovered that Quakers kept themselves busy whenever they were not occupied with worship. "The jail by that means," Penn said, "became a meeting-house and a workhouse, for they would not be idle anywhere." [28] Thomas Chalkley said: "I followed my Calling; and kept to Meetings diligently; for I was not easy to be idle; either in my spiritual or temporal Callings." [29]

Frugality was often recommended on religious grounds as being essential to the austere simplicity of life that truth demanded. It was also justified on practical grounds as tending to increase one's capital and credit. For example, Isaac Norris, a well-known Quaker merchant, advised his son: "Thou must remember that the more frugal thou art the more will be thy Stock. . . . Come back plain, this will be a reputation to thee and recommend thee to the best and most Sensible people." [30]

QUAKER HONESTY

Each Quaker was examined in a two-fold manner. There was a continual examination of oneself through introspection— letting the Inner Light speak to the individual, correcting him at each step of the way. An outward examination took place at the meeting house when regular queries of the members were made. Questions such as "Are Friends careful to live within the Bounds of their Circumstances, and to avoid launching into Trade or Business beyond their ability to manage?" were asked.[31] Thus, the Quaker merchant was disciplined with consequences not only for his honesty, but for social order as well. If one mismanaged his business, he was in danger of disapproval, almost amounting to excommunication. No Quaker could afford to be disowned by the meeting. This fear of censure further reinforced the Quaker in doing his best to carry on his business in a diligent, honest, and prudent manner.

Quaker honesty and dependability became a byword with the non-Quaker community. Quaker businessmen could be trusted. The Quakers set higher standards on their goods than any outside agency demanded. George Fox could say with confidence: "When people came to have experience of Friend's honesty and faithfulness, and found that their yea was yea and their nay was nay; that they kept to a word in their dealings, and that they would not cozen and cheat them."[32] It is little wonder then that customers preferred to do business with such merchants.

Although they established a reputation as reliable merchants, the Quakers were often suspected of being shrewd, conniving, sly, and dishonest. There was the inevitable jealousy on the part of those who could not understand the secret of the Quaker business acumen. That the Quakers were honest, truthful, and simple did not mean that they were stupid. Trade secrets and valuable market information was not divulged in a naive manner to strangers. If speech was silver, silence was golden. An experienced Quaker merchant, John Reynell, counseled young Elias Bland thus:

> In doing business be a little on the Reserve, and Observe well the Person thou has to do with. . . . Keep thy Business to thy self, and don't let it be known, who thou dost Business for, or what Sorts of Goods thou Ships off. Some will want to know both, perhaps with a Design to Circumvent thee. Endeavour to know what Prices other People give for Goods, but Say nothing of what thou gives thy self,— or where thou Buys, its very Probable some will tell thee, they give more for a thing than they did, on Purpose to make thee buy dear, in Order to do thee an Injury in thy Business. If thou finds out a Place where they Sell cheap, keep it to thy Self, for if thou Ships off Goods cheaper than others, it will increase business.[33]

It is not surprising that the uncommunicative Quaker, who found that it "paid" to be close-mouthed, seemed secretive and subtle, and how, consequently, the traits of slyness and dishonesty could be built into the legend of the Quaker businessman.[34] Jean Pierre Brissot de Warville, a Frenchman who visited Philadelphia in 1788, summarized the Quakers thus: "The order which the Quakers are accustomed from childhood to apply to the distribution of their tasks, their thoughts, and every moment of their lives. They carry this spirit of order everywhere; it economizes time, activity, and money." Brissot added that this is quite different from the training and habits customary in Catholic France.[35]

Tolles undoubtedly had Max Weber in mind when he comments upon Brissot's observation of the Quakers in these words: "This virtue was essential for success in a 'rationalized' capitalist economy in which the pursuit of gain was regarded as a continuous and intensive activity based upon the expectation of regular production, markets, and profits."[36] These virtues were not accidental but deliberately cultivated as may be seen from William Penn's letters to his children in which he advised them to cultivate the habit of order, suggesting that they set aside a part of each day for meditation and worship of God, a part for business, and a part for themselves.[37]

CONDUCT OF BUSINESS

Obtaining credit in England for the purchase of manufactured goods was a persistent problem in Pennsylvania. The problem arose because there was no market in Great Britain for the natural products of the Philadelphia region. Hence, it was necessary to work out the schemes of triangular or polygonal trade whereby local exports could be exchanged for commodities marketable in the mother country.[38] Quaker John Reynell summarizes the solutions in these words:

> We make our Remittances a great many different ways sometimes to the West Indies in Bread, Flour, Pork, Indian Corn, and hogshead Staves, sometimes to Carolina and Newfoundland in Bread and Flour sometimes to Portugall in Wheat, Flour and Pipe Staves sometimes to Ireland in Flax Seed Flour, Oak and Walnut Planks, Boat Boards, Pigg Iron, Tarr, Pitch, Turpentine, Ships, and Bills of Exchange.[39]

The Quaker merchants dealt in a variety of products, such as rice, logwood, pitch, tar, turpentine, sugar, cocoa, indigo, ginger, pimentos, Madeira, muscovado sugar, and lime. Some merchants sold their wares at public auction using unscrupulous methods and defrauding people unmercifully, often getting them drunk to encourage rash bidding. The Yearly Meeting of 1726 protested these abuses and enacted a statute officially providing for appointed vendue masters who were bonded for the faithful performance of their duties.[40]

Non-Quakers frequently accused Quakers of prospering by virtue of "Keeping their Trade within themselves and maintaining a strict Correspondence and Intelligence over all parts where they are." This accusation, in Tolles' opinion, was to a large measure correct. Quakers believed in mutual aid. They cooperated from all parts of the world reinforcing their fellowship by corresponding with other meetings. This practice has been followed to the present day, as may be seen from an examination of the *Proceedings of the Yearly Meetings of the Religious Society of Friends* issued each year.

Frequently when Philadelphia Quakers traveled abroad, the merchants with whom they had business dealings were almost exclusively Quakers. These included some of the greatest traders in the metropolis such as Henry Gouldney, Daniel Flexney, Sampson Lloyd, David Barclay, John Asquew, Joseph Hoar, Issac Hunt, and Andrew Pitt (immortalized in Voltaire's *Lettres Philosophiques*).[41]

Quakers lacked confidence in the joint-stock company as an instrument of trade. Partnerships and single proprietorships were preferred. These were usually agreements within the family. If this was impossible, someone from the Quaker Meeting was selected. Apprentices were carefully selected and trained in the virtues of Quaker business methods.

The perpetual problem of making remittances to England forced the Philadelphia merchants to purchase on credit, although this was avoided whenever possible. The Quakers heeded the Book of Discipline that warned against launching into business beyond one's ability. They did their best not to order merchandise from England without possessing the cash for the remittance. "In the conduct of business, the Quaker merchants were extremely cautious and prudent, meticulously accurate in details, and insistent upon others being so. It is not difficult to understand how men who exhibited these traits in their commercial dealings should have acquired a reputation for driving a hard bargain." [42]

Quakers extended their efforts to real estate and to mining and manufacturing enterprises. Samuel Carpenter, for example, possessed much valuable real estate in Philadelphia. It included mansions, two warehouses, a tavern, a coffeehouse, a long wharf, a large estate in Philadelphia, and a thousand additional acres lying around "Pickering mine." Issac Norris called Carpenter "that honest and valuable man whose industry and improvements have been the stock whereon much of the labours and successes of this country have been grafted." [43]

Leading Quaker merchants continued to believe in the philosophy that "commonly people become wealthy by sobriety and industry, the most useful qualifications in a commonwealth, and poor by luxury, idleness and folly." [44] A leading Quaker merchant, James Logan, attributed widespread poverty to idleness, love of pleasure, and the perverse refusal of workmen to labor for reasonable wages. Logan said further:

> They grow factious and turbulent in the State; for trying new Politics. . . . They are for Inventing and Ease: When it is certain, that nothing can prove Truly Effectual to them, but a change of their own Measures in the Exercise of those wholesome and healing Virtues . . . *Sobriety, Industry, and Frugality.*[45]

Thus, on the whole, the Quaker merchants continued to accumulate material wealth. The two strains in their economic ethic—"the individualist-capitalist and the radical human-itarian—tended to diverge, each finding expression in differ-ent persons."[46]

SUMMARY

In spite of hostility on the part of the ruling classes and opposition from the established church and the king, through energy, honesty, and native ability the Quakers achieved prosperity and a degree of influence far beyond what might have been expected from a small group. Their industrial activities were widespread in weaving, shipping, pottery making, pharmaceutical manufacture, the manufacture of scientific instruments, and clock making. Their reputation for probity led many people to deposit their savings with them at a time when banks were virtually nonexistent. Be-cause of their refusal to take oaths, they could enter neither universities nor political life in England. Their pacifism pre-vented them from entering the armed forces. Therefore they utilized their talents in trade and commerce, migrating to the cities rather than remaining in the rural areas.

Their mysticism served to prepare them for an active participation in the events of the world. While they accepted the ethical code of the Anabaptists, they rejected their monastic inclinations. By laboring diligently in their chosen calling, Quakers expected the Lord to bestow His blessings in material form. Living austerely in accordance with "Simplicity and Truth," they accumulated wealth for "the Honour of God and Good of Mankind." Each Quaker had to search his own heart and in addition had to answer to fellow members in the Business Meeting. Honesty was always considered to be the best policy. From childhood, they were taught to apply order to the distribution of their tasks, their thoughts, and every moment of their lives.

In the conduct of their businesses, Quakers cooperated with other Quakers, receiving reports from all over the world regarding prevailing prices. Normally, they entered into partnerships within the family. Where this was not possible, a Quaker, approved by the business meeting, was accepted. They prospered in real estate, mining, and manufacturing enterprises. Their business philosophy at all times called for the virtues of sobriety, industry, and frugality. They set aside a definite part of each day for meditation and worship of God, a part for business, and a part for themselves. While it is not possible to measure the extent of their spiritual gain, history does indicate that the Quakers most assuredly accumulated an abundance of material wealth.

NOTES

1. From "The Advice of William Penn to His Children," *Works*, I, as cited by Frederick B. Tolles, *Meeting House and Counting House* (Chapel Hill, N. C., 1948), p. 45.

2. Giovanni Paolo Marana, "Letters Writ by a Turkish Spy," *Gentleman's Magazine,* vol. 6 (London, 1801).

3. Tolles, *Meeting House and Counting House,* p. 47.

4. Ibid.

5. Ibid., p. 48.

6. Gerald Beekman to Samuel Fowler, December 1761, quoted in Virginia D. Harrington, *The New York Merchant on the Eve of the Revolution* (New York, 1935), p. 229.

7. Tolles, *Meeting House and Counting House,* p. 49.

8. Ibid., p. 50.

9. Werner Sombart, *The Quintessence of Capitalism,* trans. M. Epstein (London, 1915), p. 287.

10. Amelia M. Gummere, *The Quaker in the Forum* (Philadelphia, 1910), p. 41.

11. George Fox, *To the Parliament of the Commonwealth of England* (London, 1659), p. 5.

12. Thomas Clarkson, *A Portraiture of Quakerism* (New York, 1806), 2:42.

13. Tolles, *Meeting House and Counting House,* p. 50.

14. Ibid., p. 64.

15. Ernst Troeltsch, *Social Teaching of the Christian Churches,* trans. Olive Wyon (London & New York, 1931), 2:915.

16. Richard B. Schlatter, *The Social Ideas of Religious Leaders, 1660–1688* (London, 1940), p. 235.

17. Tolles, *Meeting House and Counting House,* p. 6.

18. Ibid., p. 9.

19. William Penn, "No Cross No Crown" (1669) in *Works* (Philadelphia, 1792), 1:295, 296.

20. George Fox, "The Line of Righteousness and Justice Stretched Forth over All Merchants," *Works* (1661) 1:197.

21. Perry Miller, *The New England Mind* (New York, 1939), p. 42.

22. "Letter to John Pemberton," 7 June 1749, *Pemberton Papers,* ed. Thomas Wilkinson (London, 1810), 5:107.

23. Tolles, *Meeting House and Counting House,* p. 55.

24. "An additional Extract from Other of George Fox's Epistles," *Works,* 7:345.

25. Penn, "No Cross No Crown," p. 295.

26. Thomas Chalkley, "A Journal or Historical Account of the Life, Travels, and Christian Experiences of that Antient, Faithful Servant of Jesus Christ," in *A Collection of the Works of Thomas Chalkley* (Philadelphia, 1749), pp. 97–98.

27. Letter to J. Askew, 9 July 1717, in "Letter Books," in *Logan Papers* (Philadelphia, 1927), 4:37.

28. Tolles, *Meeting House and Counting House,* p. 57.

29. Chalkley, "Account of the . . . Faithful Servant," passim.

30. Tolles, *Meeting House and Counting House,* p. 58.

31. Quoted in Tolles, *Meeting House and Counting House,* p. 59. From "The Book of Discipline as Revised by the Yearly Meeting for Pennsylvania and New Jersey in the Year 1719," manuscript in Friends Historical Library of Swarthmore College, pp. 15, 76.

32. George Fox, *Journal,* I, passim.

33. Letter dated 22 June 1743, "Reynell Letter Book," Coates-Reynell Papers, Originally published in *The Friend* (Philadelphia, 1927).

34. Tolles, *Meeting House and Counting House,* p. 61.

35. Jean Pierre Brissot de Warville, *Nouveau voyage dans les Etats-unis de l'Amerique septentrionale,* vol. 2, as cited in Tolles, *Meeting House and Counting House,* p. 61.

36. Ibid.

37. William Penn, "Advice to his Children," in *Works,* 1:899.

38. Tolles, *Meeting House and Counting House,* p. 86.

39. "Letter to Thomas Smith," Sept. 4, 1741, *Reynell Letter Book,* 1738–1741, as cited in Tolles, *Meeting House and Counting House,* p. 87.

40. Tolles, *Meeting House and Counting House,* p. 89.

41. Ibid., p. 91.

42. Ibid., p. 95.

43. Ibid., p. 97.

44. Norris quoted by Tolles, ibid., p. 104.

45. Logan quoted by Tolles, ibid., p. 105.

46. Ibid., p. 106.

PART THREE

THE JAINS
OF INDIA

5

A SHORT HISTORY OF JAINISM

Jainism, like Buddhism, arose as a reaction against Hinduism. Originally a heterodox Hindu sect, it evolved as a mode of perfecting a basic Hindu ideal. Buddhism and Jainism both sprang up in the classical period of ancient India (500–300 B.C.) as a solution to the central problems of Indian life. Every religious Hindu was deeply concerned with the problem of never-ending rebirth. The concept of samsara rested on the belief in the transmigration of souls. The soul of a man at death is believed to pass into another existence, except in the case of one who at death became unusually holy and merged with Brahma. Depending upon one's merits, successive rebirths could be on a higher or a lower plane. A man of low caste could be reborn into a noble family or vice versa. The law of karma decides man's fate; everything a man does, his thoughts, deeds and actions, are thought to have fateful consequences. "Thou art weighed in the balances and art found wanting," [1] could be true of any man. "Whatsoever

a man soweth that shall he also reap" [2] meant to the Hindu
that if a man were born a Shudra (non-Aryan servant), it
was because he had sinned in his previous existence. A
passage in the *Chandogya Upanishad* states: "Those who are
of pleasant conduct here, the prospect is, indeed, that they
will enter a pleasant womb, either the womb of a Brahmin,
or the womb of a Kshytriya, or the womb of a Vaisya. But
those who are of a stinking conduct here, the prospect is,
indeed, that they will enter either the womb of a swine,
or the womb of an outcast." [3]

Hinduism permitted a wide latitude of beliefs. One could
be monotheistic, polytheistic, pantheistic, monistic, dualistic,
pluralistic. One could attend a temple or stay at home and
follow a loose or strict moral conduct. However, each person
was required to follow the rules of his caste; doing so was
equivalent to being a righteous man and earning credit in
the life hereafter.[4]

By about the end of the seventh century B.C., ancient Indian
society was in ferment. Four distinct social groups were recognized at this time: the Kshatriyas or warriors; the Brahmans,
the priests; the Vaisyas, the traders; and the Shudras, the
non-Aryan servants. In old Aryan conquest territory, the
Kshatriya aristocrats and kings utilized the Brahmans to
legitimize their power. By this time, all people held the
sacred prayer formulas recited by the Brahmans at the time
of the sacrifice as extremely important for success in life.
The Kshatriyas, who implored the Brahmans to use these
formulas before facing the enemy, were led to believe by
the Brahmans that success was the result of their intercession
to the Brahma; the Brahmans claimed that they alone had the
prerogative to utter the sacred formulas. Eventually, the

Brahman priests declared openly that they occupied the central place of power. They had compiled the *Brahmanas* (scripture containing detailed instruction for ritual performances), and by proper use of these they were in a position to procure the desired results. By about 500 B.C. the caste system solidified in the following hierarchical order: the Brahmans, the Kshatriyas, the Vaisyas, and finally the Shudras. These last, outside the pale of this social structure, were the "untouchables" or outcasts. Innumerable subcastes were formed within each caste.

The states of northern India were at the time "Aryanized" to varying degrees (that is, brought under the domination of Aryan princes). In the predominantly agricultural states of northeast India, the royal families sponsored the heterodox religions as a weapon against the Brahmans.

Many people were disturbed by the theory propagated by the Brahmans that the reason they found themselves in the highest category of the social structure was the result of the law of karma; that is, they had done well in their previous birth and had had the good fortune of being born a Brahman, a precondition to mergence with the Brahma, the ultimate reality. The Brahmans argued that because they had a record of superior spiritual attainment, they deserved the highest position. Although there was considerable resistance from the Kshatriyas, they had no notion of contradicting the doctrine of transmigration and the consequences of karma in determining one's destiny. Lacking any weighty counter-argument, they had to content themselves with second place.[5] Some were prepared to concede reluctantly to the Brahmans the social prestige of being at the top in the caste system. Others questioned the necessity for a person to be born a Brahman before being permitted to merge himself with the Brahma, the ground of all reality whether objective or subjective. Heroic efforts were made by the founders of Jainism, later followed by those of Buddhism, to find a way out of this dilemma.

Hinduism was based on the conviction that the chief error of man lies in his thinking that his miseries are due to fallacies in his concept of things rather than to his sinning. Early Buddhism located the chief missteps in the area of feeling. Jainism, a religion that arose as a reaction against the Brahmanical doctrine of salvation limited to persons born into the Brahman caste, placed the primary emphasis on behavior, on how one acts. One must behave in such a way as to avoid contamination by matter, considered as defiling as pitch and destructive of all spirituality of being.[6]

In the Occident it is commonly believed that Vardhamana Mahavira, a contemporary of Gautama Buddha, was the founder of Jainism. Traditionally, however, the Jains regarded Mahavira not as the first but the last of the Tirthankaras, the Jain prophets. Undoubtedly, several of the Tirthankaras were mythological. Still, according to the Jainologist Heinrich Zimmer, there is sufficient ground to accept the authenticity of Parsvanatha, "the Lord Parsva," who is alleged to have attained liberation 246 years before Mahavira. The Jains have such profound respect for Parsva that we read in one passage: "At the mere mention of the name of the Lord Parsva disturbances cease, the sight [*darsana*] of him destroys the fear of rebirths, and his worship removes the guilt of sin." [7]

The Tirthankaras or the Makers of the River-Crossing are not to be worshipped, although they may be contemplated.

They are believed beyond the reach of intercession. They have reached the state of nirvana, that is, enlightenment through forfeiture of desires, and have passed beyond the godly governors of the natural order. Hence, Zimmer regards Jainism not as atheistic but as transtheistic. The Tirthankaras are supposed to be beyond cosmic events. They are transcendent, omniscient, actionless, and absolutely at peace. The Jain is expected to exercise ascetic discipline and contemplate passing the Tirthankaras. These practices assist him in passing beyond needs and anxieties to prayer, "and beyond the blissful heavens in which those gods and their worshippers abide, into the remote, transcendent, 'cut-off' zone of pure, uninflicted existence to which the Crossing-Makers, the Tirthankaras, have cleaved the way." [8]

The adherents of Mahavira regard him to be the twenty-fourth Tirthankara. Parsva, his predecessor, was the twenty-third, having obtained nirvana 246 years before Mahavira did.[9] Although reliable dates are not available, some authorities, including Zimmer, accept 772 B.C. as the probable date of the attainment of nirvana by Parsva, assigning 526 B.C. as the probable date for this attainment by Mahavira.

The concept of the transmigration of souls was rarely, if ever, questioned by any of the religious thinkers of the day. Until the achievement of nirvana, rebirth followed rebirth. Nirvana was not at all easy to obtain. Jain lore maintains that Bhagwan Aristanemi, the predecessor of Parsva, had achieved this state eighty-four thousand years ago. The saints were few and far between, but their biographies served as models for all to follow.[10]

The trials and tribulations of the saints were conceived to inspire the followers to take heart and to be faithful unto the end. Nirvana is not limited to the Buddhist idea, as is commonly supposed. It existed long before the Buddhists made it popular. (Literally, *nirva* means "to blow out; to cease to draw breath"; *nirvana* means "blown out"—the fire of desire quenched and pacified.) The Jain idea of nirvana may be understood best by Zimmer's account of the manner in which Parsvanatha attained it:

> He had been dwelling and ruling as an Indra in the thir-
> teenth heaven when his time to re-enter the world of men
> arrived and he descended to the womb of Queen Vama,
> the beautiful consort of King Asvasena. All who beheld
> the child as he grew to manhood were amazed by his beauty
> and strength, delights, and temptations of the palace.
> Neither his father's noble throne nor female loveliness
> could hold his interest; all that he ever desired was to
> renounce the world. Unwillingly the family consented to
> the departure of the prince, and the gods at that moment
> descended to celebrate the "Great Renunciation." They
> transported him in a heavenly palanquin to the forest,
> where he took his vow of *sannyasa:* irrevocable decision
> to annihilate his moral nature. . . . Thereafter, as a Tirthan-
> kara, a living savior, he taught and moved among mankind.
> And when he had fulfilled his earthly mission, being then
> one hundred years of age, his life-monad became separated
> from its earthly coil and rose to the ceiling of the universe,
> where it now abides forever.[11]

Following the traditional belief in the transmigration of souls, the biographies contained a mythological account of the earlier births—when the saint existed on lower levels, such as insects and animals—thus a gradual progression could be seen up to the final achievement of complete liberation. This was portrayed not only for the Hindu saints but also for the Jain and Gautama Buddha himself. The struggle between good and evil, light and darkness, is constant. Eventually, the struggle between the darker brother and the brother who portrays light and all that is desirable ends in victory for the latter.[12]

THE FOUNDER OF MODERN JAINISM

For our purpose it is not necessary to dwell at length upon the life of Parsva; let it suffice to say that Mahavira, though not the sole founder of Jainism, may be credited as the founder of modern Jainism. He was undoubtedly helped by the existence of a religious community of monks sympathetic to the teachings of Parsva and his predecessors.[13] Mahavira (literally, "Great Hero"), was the charismatic leader of Jainism. We are fortunate that he lived in a period when the deeds of men were generally well documented, for India at this time was passing through a period of intellectual ferment. It is interesting to note that like the earlier Jain prophets or Tirthankaras, Mahavira was not of the Brahman stock. Like his contemporary, the Buddha, he was born into a Kshatriya family.[14] His home was in the Jnata clan in Kundagrama (*kunda*=a pit, *grama*=a village), a suburb of Vaisali in the northeastern province of Bihar. The son of a Kshatriya nobleman, his parents, Siddharta and Trisala, were very pious Jains who worshipped Parsva. Being their second son, he was named Vardhamana (literally, "growing and increasing"). In due course he married Yasoda and a daughter was born called Anojja. When his parents died he was in his thirtieth year. Legend has it that he requested that his guardian and older brother, Nandavirdhana, permit him to

renounce the world and become a monk and that this permission was readily granted. There was nothing unusual
about becoming a monk, and to the delight of Vardhamana
he qualified in the eyes of the leader of the order and was
received into their fellowship.

For the next twelve years Mahavira practiced self-mortifi-
cation, the severity of which may be realized from legend,
where it is said that after the first twelve months he had to
discard all his clothes as part of his initiation; he retired
from the world. He "plucked out with his right and left
hands on the right and left sides of his head, his hair in
five handfuls." The pledge he took before the monks was
as follows: "I shall neglect my body and abandon the care
of it; I shall with equanimity bear, undergo, and suffer all
calamities arising from divine powers, men, or animals."[15]
After a long ordeal he achieved the state of kevala, which
is similar to the state of complete "isolation integration"
and may be likened to the bodhi, the enlightenment of the
Buddhists. Living a strict, austere life did not satisfy the
spiritual thirst of Mahavira, and he set out clad only in
atmosphere, to seek complete moksha—release from the cycle
of rebirth.

The Jains had long ago been offended by the doctrines
of the Brahmans and believed that it was possible for non-
Brahmans to achieve complete release. For forty-two years
after leaving the company of his fellow monks, Mahavira
wandered throughout North India, preaching his doctrines
—known as the gandhara—and instructing his eleven chief
disciples. He died at Pava, not far from Patna, having attained
final release or nirvana at the age of seventy-two. Faithful
Jains make a pilgrimage to Pava whenever possible. Accord-

ing to the Svetambara sect, he died in 527 B.C., while according to the Digambaras, it was in 509 B.C.; in the Occident it
is regarded to be 480 B.C. In any event, Mahavira died just a
few years before Buddha.[16]

He held two firm convictions: first, that absolute asceticism
was essential to save one's soul from all evil, that is, to purge
contaminating matter from the soul; and, secondly, that maintaining the purity and integrity of one's own soul involves
the ceaseless practice of noninjury (ahimsa) to any and all
living beings. Mahavira was indeed an embodiment of extreme asceticism and the practice of ahimsa. Legend records
that he never stayed for more than one night in any one
place; he was literally afraid of forming any emotional attachment to any place that might bind him to the world and its
people. Only during the heavy monsoon season did he remain
in the same place, and then not because travel would have
involved discomfort, but rather because the roads and paths
were teeming with life and the practice of ahimsa required
remaining quiescent.[17] The unusual precautions Mahavira
took may be understood from a passage taken from the
Gaina Sutras:

> Thoroughly knowing the earth-bodies and water-bodies and
> fire-bodies and wind-bodies, the lichens, seeds, and sprouts,
> he comprehended that they are, if narrowly inspected, im-
> bued with life, and avoided to injure them. . . . Walking
> he meditated with his eyes fixed on a square space before
> him of the length of a man. . . . Looking a little sideward,
> looking a little behind, attentively looking on his path (he
> did not wish to step on any living thing). Many sorts of
> living beings gathered on his body, crawled about it and
> caused pain there. (He did not scratch himself.) Without
> ceasing in his reflections, the Venerable One slowly wan-

dered about, and, killing no creatures, he begged for his food.[18]

Further examination of the *Gaina Sutras* reveals that Mahavira took great precautions to sweep the path he trod lest he injure the insects; he examined the bed to see that no eggs or living insects were present.[19] The food that he ate was first examined to see if it was free from worms or even mildew; these were carefully removed and only the remainder was consumed. Because Mahavira was the founder of modern Jainism, it will be useful to examine another passage in connection with extreme asceticism:

> This is the rule followed by the Venerable One: When the cold season has halfway advanced, the houseless one, leaving off his robe and stretching out his arms, should wander about, not leaning against a tree-trunk. . . . When a cold wind blows, in which some feel pain, then some houseless monks in the cold rain seek a place sheltered from the wind. "We shall put on more clothes; kindling wood, or well covered, we shall be able to bear the very influence of the cold." But the Venerable One desired nothing of the kind; strong in control, he suffered, despising all shelter. . . . Sometimes in the cold season the Venerable One was meditating in the shade. In summer he [exposed] himself to the heat, he [sat] squatting in the sun. The Venerable One did not seek sleep for the sake of pleasure; he waked up himself, and slept only a little. . . . Purgatives and emetics, anointing of the body, and bathing, shampooing, and cleansing of the teeth do not behoove him.[20]

Detachment was preferable to attachment. With this thought in mind, Mahavira refrained from speaking to or greeting anyone. This earned him a great deal of ill-will from inquisitive villagers, but he bore all affronts with determined indifference.[21] Another passage reads:

For some it is not easy to do what he did, not to answer those who salute; he was beaten with sticks, and struck by sinful people. Giving up the company of all householders whomsoever, he meditated. Asked, he gave no answer. Disregarding slights difficult to bear, the Sage wandered about, not attracted by story-tellers, pantomimes, songs, fights at the quarter-staff, and boxing matches. . . . The dogs bit him, ran at him. Few people kept off the attacking, biting dogs. Striking the monk, they cried "Khukkhu," and made the dogs bite him. . . . When he once sat without moving his body, they cut his flesh, tore his hair, covered him with dust. Throwing him up, they let him fall, or disturbed him in his religious postures; abandoning the care of his body, the Venerable One humbled himself.[22]

Mahavira followed this rigorous routine meticulously for a full twelve years. Through this invincible self-discipline, he at last secured his heart's desire; he attained moksha, the liberation he had set out to achieve. Henceforth he had a message for those around him. The *Gaina Sutras* have recorded the event in vivid terms:

During the thirteenth year, in the second month of summer, in the fourth fortnight . . . when the shadow had turned toward the east . . . outside the town Gimbhikagrama, on the northern bank of the river Rigupalika, in the field of the householder Samaga, in a northeastern direction from an old temple, not far from a sal tree, in a squatting position, with knees high and head low, in deep meditation, in the midst of abstract meditation, he reached Nirvana, the complete and full . . . called Kevala.[23]

Having obtained this liberation of victory, he became a true jina (a victorious person or a conqueror). For the remainder of his life, thirty more years, he propagated his faith and won many disciples. Eventually, at the age of seventy-two, his moksha included even liberation from physical existence; he ascended to the Jain heaven called Isatpragbhara. Henceforth the followers, too, could become victorious and thus claim the title of Jain.

THE RELIGIOUS DOCTRINES
OF THE JAINS

Jainism and Buddhism both developed as a challenge to Hinduism. While Buddhism spread to Ceylon, Burma, Cambodia, Siam, China, Japan, Korea, Tibet (Lamaism), and Mongolia, where it became the national religion, it was not successful in India, its home. Jainism, on the other hand, failed to spread abroad, though it took a strong hold in India and today is the faith of 1.6 million people. The world, during the time of Mahavira and Buddha, was in great intellectual ferment. It was the period of the early Greek philosophers, the Old Testament prophets, Confucius in China, and possibly Zarathustra in Persia; in India particular agitation was stirred as Hinduism was challenged by intellectual, non-Brahman sons of the soil.

In addition to the strong intellectual climate, there were other reasons for faiths such as Jainism and Buddhism to make inroads into Hinduism at this time. Don Martindale, a contemporary social theorist, has summarized the state of India at this time:

> During the time that the Indian world was being transformed from one of semifeudal manorial communities to loosely knit kingdoms comprising a series of forms varying from peasant villages to thriving cities, the Brahmans were in a strategic position to monopolize the intellectual roles. . . . The Brahmans infiltrated the learned occupations,

particularly administrative posts, which demanded writing skill and education, as did the clerics of the Middle Ages. However, the restrictive monopolies of the Brahmans and the groups they represented met with serious resistance from the kings. Resistance was particularly strong in the kingdoms east of the lands where the Brahmans enjoyed traditional strength. In the course of the sixth century B.C., both the Buddhists and Jain orders took shape in this area.[24]

The extent to which the life of the Jain ascetic was modeled after the Brahman has been shown by Jacobi's comparison of the rules of the two disciplines. However, as Martindale points out, though the Jain monks were responding to the same role requirements as the Brahmans, they offered a different solution.[25] Traditionally in India the stories connected with the birth of a religious leader had always given a clue to his future greatness; the birth story of the founder of Jainism, Mahavira, was intended to show that it was a greater honor to be born of a Kshatriya than of a Brahman mother. Similarly, the birth story of Buddha, the founder of Buddhism, has the same point in view. Mrs. Stevenson, author of *The Rites of the Twice-Born,* has observed that throughout the Jain sacred books, antagonism to the Brahmans is evident in such matters as bathing, divination, and sacrifice (as may be seen from the life of Mahavira). The Brahmans stress the importance of caste, whereas the Jains place emphasis on man's behavior; to the Jain, man's actions have ethical consequence. Not only Mahavira, but his successors and disciples were primarily drawn from the ranks of the Kshatriya.[26] It is not surprising to discover that Mahavira and his successors were well received at the courts of the Rajas in the kingdom of Magadha. The common Kshatriya background was a natural link between the rulers and the religious leaders of Jainism.

In order to understand and estimate the influence, if any, of contemporary teachers of Mahavira upon the Jain doctrines, it would be well to consider very briefly the leading doctrines of the heterodox teachers of the day. The Buddhist scriptures mention at least six unorthodox teachers in *Digha Nikaya*. A. L. Basham has observed that there was Purana Kassapa, an antinomian, who believed that virtuous conduct had no effect on a man's karma: "He who performs an act . . . [he who, for instance] destroys life [or] commits adultery . . . [actually] commit[s] no sin. . . . From liberality, self-control, abstinence, and honesty is derived neither merit nor the approach of merit." [27]

The second heretic was Makkhali Gosala who agreed with Purana that good deeds did not affect transmigration which proceeded according to a rigid pattern, controlled by an all powerful cosmic principle which he called niyati (fate): "No human action, no strength, no courage, no human endurance . . . can affect one's destiny in this life." [28]

The third teacher was Ajita Kesakambala, a materialist. "When the body dies both fool and the wise alike are cut off and perish. They do not survive after death . . . [hence] there is no merit in almsgiving, sacrifice, or offering, no result or ripening of good or evil deeds." [29]

The fourth was Pakudha Kacchayana, an atomist who lived a century before Democritus but developed a similar doctrine of eternal atoms. "The seven elementary categories are neither made nor ordered, neither caused nor constructed; they are barren, as firm as mountains. . . . Even if a man cleave another's head with a sharp sword, he does not take life, for the sword-cut passes between the seven elements." [30]

The fifth heretical teacher was Vardhamana Mahavira. A

total of seven known systems (including Buddhism and Brahmanism) were available for an Indian to follow; most of them, however, faded in the course of time. Buddhism spread abroad while Jainism lodged in the land of its founder where it survived the vicissitudes of over two thousand years.

THE PHILOSOPHY OF JAINISM

In India, because Jainism denies the authority of the *Vedas,* the ancient Hindu scriptures, it is regarded as a heterodox system. Jainism does not derive from Brahman-Aryan sources, but reflects the cosmology and anthropology of a much older, pre-Aryan upper class of northeastern India. Zimmer asserts that it is rooted in the same subsoil of archaic metaphysical speculation as Yoga, Sankhya, and Buddhism, which are also non-Vedic in their origin. Further, the Aryan invasion, which overwhelmed the northwestern and north central provinces of India in the second millennium B.C., did not extend its full impact beyond the middle of the Ganges Valley. For this reason, Zimmer asserts that the pre-Aryan nobility of the northeastern states were not all swept off their thrones. When the dynasties of the invading race began to show symptoms of exhaustion, the scions of these earlier native lines were able to assert themselves.[31]

While Jainism apparently uses the same technical terminology as that of Brahmanism and Buddhism, the similarity ends there since it has its own special meaning for each term —karma, matter, soul, salvation, moksha, etc. Buddhism, for example, does not accept the idea that plant life is similar to the life of a human being or that of the gods; however, with the essentially materialistic philosophy of the Jains, everything is imbued with life. There is a life-monad and it is imperishable. True, there will be innumerable stages in the experience of the individual—he may at one stage be a plant, animal, insect, god or human—but there is a continuity in the chain of events. The sense faculties, possessed by humans or gods, are the reasoning faculty (manas), span of life (ayusha), physical strength (kaya-bala), faculty of speech (vakya-bala), and power of respiration (svasocchvasa-bala). Those animals which lack the reasoning faculty are "insensible" (a-sanjiin); these would include fish, frogs, etc. The brighter animals such as elephants, lions and cows, like humans, are classified as sanjiin.[32]

Karma matter continues to accumulate during the course of one's life, forming successive layers on the individual. Karma matter pervades the body of a person and, in some inexplicable manner, communicates various colors; each layer has its own peculiar color. In the ascending order they are as follows:

6. white (sukla)
5. yellow, or rose (padma; literally, "lotus")
4. flaming red (tejas)
3. dove grey (kapota)
2. dark blue (nila)
1. black (krsna)

Black is the characteristic color of merciless, cruel, raw people representing things that are harmful; dark blue represents covetousness, greed, sensuality, and fickleness; dove grey typifies recklessness and thoughtlessness; the prudent are represented by fiery red; yellow depicts compassion; the white souls are dispassionate, absolutely disinterested, and impartial.[33]

All the thoughts and deeds of an individual, be they good or evil, form a tenacious karma matter that decides the existence of a person in the next life. Everything is determined by a person's actions—his nationality, his earthly span, his membership in a caste; thus, karma matter affects the entire future life. Everything is eternal and classified in two categories. Ajiva consists of everything that is lifeless, yet permanent—dead matter. Jiva, on the other hand, is full of life and of definite value; all desirable qualities are relegated to this category. The existence of Brahma-Atman (the ground of all reality) is denied. Contrary to the teachings of the Brahmans, there is no supreme ruler of the universe. Mahavira was a pluralist believing in many gods and goddesses all of them finite beings. Therefore, he could exclaim: "Man, thou art thine own friend, Why wishest thou for a friend beyond thyself?" [34] It is useless to implore the gods to act as mediators in achieving salvation. The *Vedas* are no better than mere human utterances. What must a man do to be saved? The Jains found the answer to this age-old question to be asceticism of the severest kind.

The following code, called the "Five Great Vows," was to serve as a guide for the monks in their practice of asceticism:

> 1. *Ahimsa:* I renounce all killing of living things, whether movable or immovable. Nor shall I myself kill living beings nor cause others to do it. As long as I live I confess, and blame and exempt myself of these sins, in mind, speech, and body.

There are five clauses:

> A Nirgantha (ascetic; literally, "the undraped one") is careful in his walk, not careless.

A Nirgantha searches into his mind. If his mind is sinful, acting on impulse, produces quarrels, pains, he should not employ such a mind.

A Nirgantha searches into his speech. If his speech is sinful, produces quarrels, pains, he should not utter such speech.

A Nirgantha is careful in laying down his utensils of begging.

A Nirgantha eats and drinks after inspecting his food and drink. If a Nirgantha would eat and drink without inspecting his food and drink, he might hurt and displace or injure or kill all sorts of living beings.

On honesty or truth speaking:

2. *Asatya tyaga:* I renounce all vices of lying speech arising from anger or greed or fear or mirth. I shall neither myself speak lies nor consent to the speaking of lies by others.

Subsidiary vows include that a Nirgantha must never lose his temper, be greedy, indulge in foolish jesting.

3. *Asteya vrata:* I renounce all taking of anything not given, either in a village or a town or a wood, either a little or much, of great or small, of living or lifeless things. I shall neither take myself what is not given, nor cause others to take it, nor consent it, nor consent to their taking it.

4. *Brahmacarya vrata:* I renounce all sexual pleasure; I shall not give way to sensuality, nor cause others to do so, nor consent to it in others.

5. *Aparigraha vrata:* I renounce all attachments, whether to little or much, small or great, living or lifeless things; neither shall I myself form such attachments, nor cause others to do so, nor consent to their doing so.[35]

Women are considered to be the root of all evil. Mahavira's immortal remarks on the fairer sex are: "The greatest temptation in the world is women. . . . Men forsooth say, 'These are the vessels of happiness,' but this leads them to pain, to delusion, to death, to hell, to birth as hell-beings or brute beings." [36]

Although Mahavira was aware that these severe conditions could not be practiced by the lay followers, the general community was encouraged to strive to develop these twenty-one qualities: serious demeanor, cleanliness, good temper, striving after popularity, fear of sinning, mercy, straightforwardness, wisdom, modesty, kindliness, moderation, gentleness, care of speech, sociability, caution, studiousness, reverence for old age and old customs, humility, gratitude, benevolence, and attention to business.[37]

Since the Jain lay adherents were forbidden to take the life of a sentient creature, they might never till the soil, nor engage in butchering, fishing, brewing, or any other occupation involving the taking of life. This commandment is regarded by Noss as the most important by far in its social effect. He asserts:

It constituted a limitation that must have seemed serious to the early followers of Mahavira; but at long last it actually proved to have economic as well as religious worth, for the Jains found they could make higher profits when they turned from occupations involving direct harm to living creatures to careers in business as bankers, lawyers, mer-

chants, and proprietors of land. The other moral restrictions
of their creed, which prohibited gambling, eating meat,
drinking wine, adultery, hunting, thieving, and debauchery,
earned them social respect, and thus contributed to their
survival in the social scene.[38]

The Magadha rulers supported the Jain sect until the
Maurya dynasty came to the throne and Buddhism was given
royal preference. Great unity was maintained in the Jain
ecclesia up to 300 B.C., when, as is common in religious sects,
a split occurred. Shvetambara, the liberal sect, permitted its
followers to wear a minimum of clothing, while the
Digambaras believed in being clad in atmosphere only.[39]
Shvetambaras permitted women in their order, believing that
they too should be given an opportunity to achieve nirvana.
Digambaras continued to regard women as the root of all
evil and refused to admit women to their order. Lastly, the
Sthanakavasis became completely independent by not worshipping idols in any form, not erecting temples, and worshipping
wherever they felt inclined to do so. The form of their
worship, which involves meditation and inner introspection,
is somewhat like that of the Quakers.

For the Jains, all knowledge of the universe was relevant
to one's point of view. Every question could be answered
in the affirmative as well as in the negative; no proposition
could be absolutely true or absolutely false. Every child in
India is familiar with the story of the four blind men
examining an elephant: the elephant was like a fan, like a
big wall, like a cobra, or like a rope, depending upon the
angle of perception. Hemacandra (1088–1172), the Jain
scholar, expounded the doctrine of sayadvada which asserts
that reality is many sided; its relativism is usually expressed
by the prefix "perhaps," "maybe," or "somehow." The most

one could do was approach a statement by a series of partial ones; this provided the seven-fold formula:

1. Perhaps a thing is.
2. Perhaps it is not.
3. Perhaps it both is and is not.
4. Perhaps it is indescribable.
5. Perhaps it is and is indescribable.
6. Perhaps it is not and is indescribable.
7. Perhaps it is, is not, and is indescribable.

Jainism recognized a two-fold training—one for monks, and one for the laity. Jain monks were expected to renounce everything, while the laity was to renounce the world in principle only. The lesser vows (anu-vrata) were imposed upon the laity, which included the practice of continence, as opposed to the absolute renunciation required of the monks.

While Buddhism was contemporaneous with Jainism and like Jainism rejected the philosophy of the Brahmans, it appears that the common people preferred the "Middle Way" of Buddha to the extreme asceticism demanded by Jainism. For this reason, and probably from the impetus Buddhism received from Ashoka, the first Buddhist Emperor, Buddhism became very popular with the masses. However, as Noss states: "The paradox of their present status is, that their essentially world-renouncing religion has, in the devious course of events, secured their economic advantage among the struggling masses of India." [40]

SUMMARY

Jainism, like Buddhism, arose out of a criticism of Hinduism. Originally an anti-Hindu sect, it developed into a mode of perfecting the Hindu ideal. Hinduism was based on the conviction that the chief error of man lies in his thinking that his miseries are due to his own conceptual fallacies, rather than to sin in his life. Early Buddhism located man's error in the area of feeling; Jainism rejected this and asserted the importance of behavior. One must behave so as to avoid contamination by matter which is destructive of all spirituality of being.

The founder of modern Jainism is commonly accepted to be Vardhamana Mahavira. Mahavira, as well as many of the adherents of Jainism, was from the Kshatriya aristocracy. He organized his followers into a regular community of monks and laymen. The Jain monks took five major vows: (1) ahimsa, never to destroy any living thing; (2) asatya tyaga, denial of untruthfulness; (3) asteya vrata, never to steal; (4) brahmacharya vrata, chastity; and (5) aparigraha vrata, complete detachment from any thing or person. The Jain laymen were exhorted to develop twenty-one qualities ranging from personal cleanliness to honesty in business. In addition to the five vows, the Jain monks were expected never to eat at night, to protect all living things, to control the five senses, renounce all greed, practice forgiveness, possess high ideals, and inspect everything used to insure no insect's being injured.[41]

Jainism denies the authority of the *Vedas;* hence it is regarded as a heterodox system. It does not derive from Brahman-Aryan sources, but reflects the cosmology and the anthropology of a much older pre-Aryan upper class of northeastern India. Jainism arose as a reaction to the monastic idealism of the Brahmans, maintaining that it was not the physical world that was unreal nor the Brahma alone that was true—as the Brahmans had declared—but, rather, the physical world was actually real and the Brahma unreal. Every living thing, contended the Jains, was precious and, by extreme asceticism, one could avoid being contaminated by matter which attaches itself to humans and prevents them from achieving moksha. Further, it was not a prerequisite for a person to be born a Brahman in order to achieve nirvana.

While both Jainism and Buddhism rejected the philosophy of the Brahmans, Buddhism, which propagated the "Middle Way" for salvation, won over Jainism in the long run. Today Buddhism has spread to many countries of Southeast Asia, whereas Jainism is found only in India where less than 1 percent of the population is of Jain following.

NOTES

1. Daniel 5:27.
2. Galatians 6:7.
3. R. E. Hume, *The Thirteen Principal Upanishads* (London, 1934), p. 233.
4. The word *caste* means division and is of Portuguese origin. On arriving in India, the Portuguese in the sixteenth century found the Hindu community divided into separate groups of tribes, clans, and families, which the Hindu called castes. From this time many have accepted the traditional view that the remarkable prolification of castes in eighteenth- and nineteenth-century India was due to intermarriage and subdivision. From four primitive classes, three thousand or more castes evolved in modern India. *Caste* was applied indiscriminately to both *varna,* meaning "class," and to *jati,* meaning "caste proper." Basham states that this is a false terminology; for although castes rise and fall in the

social scale, with old castes dying out and new ones forming, the four great classes remain stable. (See A. L. Basham, *The Wonder That Was India* [New York, 1954], p. 148.) That is, caste is a development of thousands of years from the association of many different racial and other groups in a single cultural system. It is very difficult to show its origin. Traditionally, in ancient times, each varna was assigned a broad occupational field within which its members were theoretically combined. Thus, we have members of the Brahman-varna, who could be priests and teachers, Kshatriya-varna, etc. The stratification system that most directly affects the daily lives of the Indian people is jati. Occupational consciousness probably did not exist in ancient India. However, at least one Indologist, Professor Irawati Karvé, argues that the jati system existed in India prior to the arrival of the Aryans. The invaders brought with them a class system, and the two systems had to accommodate each other. See Ralph Braibanti and Joseph J. Spengler, eds., *Administration and Economic Development in India* (Durham, 1963), pp. 204–205; Irawati Karvé, *Kinship Organization in India* (Poona, 1953), p. 7.

5. John B. Noss, *Man's Religions* (New York, 1956), p. 137.

6. Ibid., p. 112.

7. Heinrich Zimmer, *Philosophies of India,* ed. Joseph Campbell (New York, 1956), p. 181.

8. Ibid., p. 182.

9. Thus it will be seen that in the Jain tradition there is no "immediate Apostolic Succession" as in the Roman Catholic Church, since many years elapsed between the liberation of Parsva and the attainment of nirvana by Vardhamana Mahavira.

10. Cf. Pauline idea, "Now all these things happened unto them for ensamples: and they are written for our admonition." I Corinthians 10:11.

11. Zimmer, *Philosophies of India,* pp. 183–185.

12. This is reminiscent of the dualism found in Zoroastrianism. It may be that pre-Aryan, Dravidian religion was rigorously moral and systematically dualistic years before the birth of Zoroaster. Joseph Campbell suggests that in Zoroastrianism a resurgence of

pre-Aryan factors in Iran followed a period of Aryan supremacy —something comparable to the Dravidian resurgence in India in the forms of Jainism and Buddhism. Of significance in this connection is the fact that the Persian "dark brother"—the tyrant Dahhak (or Azhi Dahaka)—is represented, like Parsvanatha, with serpents springing from his shoulders. See Zimmer, *Philosophies of India,* p. 186. (Both Jain and Buddhist images show the serpent over the shoulder.) Also one recalls the Old Testament stories of Cain and Abel, Esau and Jacob. (Genesis, chaps. 4, 27, 32.)

13. How far the presence of the Essenes, an ascetic Jewish sect that existed from the second century B.C. to the third century A.D., influenced and helped early Christianity is not too clear. Certain of their characteristics were found among the early Christians. The fact that Jesus attacked Pharisees and Sadducees, but never the Essenes, has been interpreted by some writers to mean that Jesus himself was an Essene. This is a moot point.

14. Zimmer, *Philosophies of India,* p. 221. Some writers, including Zimmer, regard all non-Brahman castes to be of non-Aryan stock; this is probably an extreme view.

15. Hermann Jacobi, trans., "The Gaina Sutras," in *Sacred Books of the East,* ed. F. Max Müller (Oxford, 1884), 22:200.

16. Hermann Jacobi, "The Gaina Sutras," in *Encyclopedia of Religion and Ethics,* ed. James Hastings (New York, 1955), 8:466–467.

17. Noss, *Man's Religions,* p. 144.

18. Jacobi, "The Gaina Sutras," *Sacred Books of the East,* pp. 79–80, 82, 87.

19. It is not only important that a Jain avoid killing any living thing but that he in fact support life. Thus, in Bombay a man carrying a bed full of bugs stops before a Jain home where a devout person offers three rupees (about 70¢) to the man carrying the bed, who promptly lies on it and lets the bugs feed on him. The devout Jain receives credit for this deed and the man receives sufficient money to have a square meal for the day; and, last but not least, the bug has enjoyed a sumptuous meal.

20. Jacobi, "The Gaina Sutras," *Sacred Books of the East,* pp. 82–83, 86.

21. Noss, *Man's Religions,* p. 146.

22. Jacobi, "The Gaina Sutras," *Sacred Books of the East,* pp. 80, 84–85. Cf. the view of the body in Christianity. Christ in his ministry healed the body, mended broken bones. It is "holy and acceptable to God . . . a temple of the Holy Spirit." (Romans 12:1; II Corinthians 6:16). In the life beyond, the body is raised and glorified. (Philippians 3:21).

23. Jacobi, "The Gaina Sutras," *Sacred Books of the East,* p. 201. This moksha or nirvana is not to be confused with the Hindu idea of moksha or being merged with Brahma, the ultimate reality; this takes place after death, whereas Mahavira obtained moksha while still living.

24. Don Martindale, *Social Life and Cultural Change* (New York, 1962), p. 196.

25. Ibid.

26. This is not surprising, since a Brahman felt that he was well on the way to achieving complete union with Brahma at death he saw no reason to follow the ascetic path of Mahavira.

27. A. L. Basham, *Sources of Indian Tradition, Background of Jainism and Buddhism* (New York, 1958), pp. 42–43.

28. Ibid.

29. Ibid.

30. Ibid.

31. Zimmer, *Philosophies of India,* p. 218.

32. Ibid.

33. Ibid., p. 230.

34. Jacobi, "The Gaina Sutras," *Sacred Books of the East,* p. 33.

35. Noss, *Man's Religions,* pp. 150–151.

36. Jacobi, "The Gaina Sutras," *Sacred Books of the East,* p. 21. Cf. "For the love of money is the root of all evil . . . which while some coveted after, they have pierced themselves with many sorrows." I Timothy 6:10.

37. Jarl Charpentier, *Cambridge History of India* (Cambridge, 1922), 1:224.

38. Noss, *Man's Religions,* p. 152.

39. In theory, the Tirthankaras are not supposed to contradict each other. Any apparent contradiction is always rationalized; e.g., Parsva believed that some clothes should be worn although Mahavira wore none. This is rationalized by stating that at the time of Parsva the appropriate time had not yet arrived to begin so rigorous a discipline. Cf. the practice of polygamy permitted in the Old Testament but discontinued in the New Testament period.

40. Noss, *Man's Religions,* p. 154.

41. Martindale, *Social Life and Cultural Change,* p. 197.

6

EVERYDAY
ETHIC OF
JAINISM

The principles that guide the Jains in their daily conduct are derived mainly from their religious doctrines. Although the Jains have lived in India for over two millennia, non-Jains still regard them as a peculiar people. This view is due to the way they worship, the rules of conduct they observe both for the clergy and the laity, their dietary rules, their marriage customs, their home life, their dress, language and literature, their institutions, and the manner in which they earn a livelihood and conduct their businesses.

Hindus define four objectives which they regard worth striving for, and these form the basis of their philosophy and general conduct. The first, artha, consists of material possessions or success in this life. It includes wealth, profit, success in business, or success in politics. The *Arthsastra* is the authoritative handbook on the subject. The second, kama, denotes pleasure, enjoying the fruits of love, and in general all that is pleasant and gladdens the heart. All India looks up to the Vatsyayana's *Kama-sutra* for guidance in this field. The third, dharma, defines the whole duty of man, moral as well as religious. The king's dharma is to do his kingly duties well; the Brahman's is to follow his caste regulations meticulously; the Kshatriya, the Vaisya, and the Shudra follow unwaveringly the rules of their respective castes. The *Dharma-sastras,* or Books of the Law, are the authorities on dharma. Finally, moksha is salvation or liberation and belongs to the category of soteriology.

In rejecting the doctrines of the Brahmans, Jainism changed the order of the classical fourfold aims stated above, making the fourth aim, moksha, preeminent. V. A. Sangave, a Jainologist, states:

> The rules of conduct are always designed to achieve the main aim or object in life . . . [this] is to obtain Moksha, that is freedom from the continuous cycle of births and deaths. The soul achieves real and everlasting happiness only when it can escape from *samsara* or transmigration of the soul which is always fraught with sorrows and trouble. . . . The necessary conditions to gain Moksha are *samvara* and *nirjara,* that is the stoppage of influx of Karmic matter and falling away of existing Karmic matter from the soul. Thus *samvara* and *nirjara* are the two most important milestones on the path to liberation and naturally the principles of right conduct by Jains are shaped with a view to accomplish *samvara* and *nirjara* as early as possible.[1]

The rules of conduct for laymen and the clergy are precisely laid down for the achievement of moksha. They affect every department of life.

THE JAIN WORSHIP

Jain philosophy is pluralistic, recognizing no line of demarcation between the creator and the creation. The agents of
creation are not in any way superior to their handiwork. There
are many gods and goddesses, none deserving to be worshipped more than a human being. The Jain is expected "to
work out his own salvation," but without the benefit of being
able to say, "because it is God which worketh in you both to
will and to do of His good pleasure." ² There is no short cut
to moksha. No amount of intercession by any higher being is
helpful. Long ago Mahavira said: "Man thou art thine best
friend, why seekest thou another?"

Each Jain, however, is eager to join the ranks of those
who have already become jinas (conquerors). The objects of
contemplation are not supreme beings, but those who have
already achieved nirvana. Those who have attained this ideal
are called Parameshthins.

There are five Parameshthins; among them are the Siddha
Parameshthins, who are believed to have obtained moksha,
and the Tirthankara Parameshthins, who have achieved all but
the last stage of liberation for they are still limited by their
bodies which have not been totally separated from the eternal
spirit. The Tirthankaras serve as examples to ordinary humans through this arhat-hood stage and their lives act as
guideposts to the achievement of salvation. There are still
other lesser saints for the Jains to admire and emulate.³

The Jains also worship some Hindu deities. Particular
reverence is accorded Ganesha, Skanda, Bhairava, and Hanu-
man.⁴ Mrs. Stevenson observes that Svetambaras worship
the Hindu deities more than do the Digambaras. H. V.

Glassenap, a German Jainologist, also asserts that many Jains hold in reverence sacred animals, trees, places, emblems, temples, idols, and sacred scriptures.[5] Sangave comments that with the spread of education and a revival of interest in the Jain religion, the faithful have been exhorted to keep away from such irreligious practices.[6]

The Jains erect beautiful, elaborate temples carved out of rocks, or erected on the ground, in which the idols of the Tirthankaras are found. The temple of the Jains at Mount Abu in Rajputana attracts many foreign visitors each year, as do the caves at Bijapur and Ellora.

The community appoints a pujari (priest) to be in charge of the temple. In the Digambara temples the pujari is always a Jain, while in the Svetambara temples he is normally a Hindu. In the Svetambara temples the pujari partakes in the offerings of the idol, while in the Digambara temples, the pujari, unless he is a proper Jain priest, leaves it for the temple servants.

Pious Jain couples visit the temple early each morning before eating and pay their respects to the Tirthankara. Jains often travel considerable distances to complete this daily ritual. The priest bathes the idol in milk and on special occasions in the five nectars (panchmrata). Flowers and precious sandalwood paste are placed on the idols every day.[7]

The monks and nuns are segregated in separate dwellings. From a lecture hall in the Upasraya, which roughly serves the same purpose as the Quaker Meeting House, the learned monks expound the sacred Jain texts to the laity. Here the monks and nuns counsel the Jain laymen on such vital matters as repentance and forgiveness of sins. This is known as pratikramana.

The Jain priests are expected to be as proficient in astronomy as the Hindu priests. Astrological knowledge is indispensable for guiding the laity in ascertaining the most auspicious moments for marriage ceremonies and other events.

The Jains observe several fasts during the year; the main one, paryushana, lasts ten days. On the last day, samvatsari, people break their fast and ask forgiveness of those they may have grieved during the year. During these days, Sangave observes, Jains are so zealous in preventing anyone from taking the life of an animal that they request the authorities to prohibit the slaughter of animals, and offer to repay the loss incurred with large sums of money.

As do the Hindus, the Jains have their own particular lore and superstitions. They believe that spirit beings influence human beings in spite of the fact that these spirits are themselves supposedly subject to the laws of karma. Some Jains have dabbled in magical practices and many will not undertake a journey except upon the assurance of an auspicious sign. Sangave comments that Jain superstitions have no religious sanction whatsoever.[8]

SACRAMENTS OF THE JAINS

Not only is the life of the Jain monk regulated by various ceremonies but, as Sangave comments:

> The life of a Jain layman is regulated by various ceremonies through which he has to pass right from his conception up to his death. These ceremonies are prescribed by religion with a view that a layman would lead a life in accordance with the religious principles and attain the main aim of final liberation.[9]

While the Digambaras and the Svetambaras prescribe different sacraments for their followers, the ultimate aim is always moksha. Every step of the way of a Jain is under the scrutiny of the Upasraya. The sravaka, who is a layman of the Digambara sect, ideally is expected to perform as many as fifty-two ceremonies during his lifetime. In the Jain sacred book, *Adi Purana*, the following are mentioned:

1. *Adhana* or *Garbhadhana:* Conception ceremony, performed prior to the conception of a child. At the attainment of puberty, the couple performs the prescribed rites in the temple. Only after the completion of these rites, may the couple cohabit, only at night and with a view to procreate—never for the purposes of sexual pleasure.[10]

2. *Priti:* Performed during the third month of pregnancy. Part of the worship is directed towards keeping the pregnant woman happy with worshipful music.

3. *Supriti:* The above repeated during the fifth month of pregnancy.

4. *Dhrti:* The above repeated in the seventh month of pregnancy, this time for the benefit of the unborn child.

5. *Moda:* Writing the primary letters आ सि आ ॐ सा on the body of the pregnant woman in the ninth month.

6. *Priyodbhava:* Worship at the birth of the child.

7. *Namkarma:* After the twelfth day from birth, an auspicious day is selected. After worship, the child is given one of the 1008 names of jina.

8. *Bahiryana:* The child is taken out of the house after three or four months on an auspicious day.

9. *Nishadya:* The child is made to sit after duly performing a ceremony.

10. *Annaprasana:* Feeding the child after proper prayers during the eighth month.

11. *Vyushti:* Worship and fast performed at the child's first anniversary.

12. *Kesvapa:* Child's head is shaved for the first time.

13. *Lipisankhyanasangraha:* In the fifth year after appropriate ceremony, the child is taught the art of writing at the hands of a learned layman.

14. *Upanti:* This is the initiation ceremony performed at the age of eight in the temple. The child wears the sacred thread, takes the five small vows, is known as a Brahmachari or a celibate. From now on maintains himself by begging alms.

15. *Vratacharya:* The child keeps his vows, maintains celibacy, and studies at the feet of his teachers.

16. *Vratavatarana:* About the age of sixteen, the child ceases to be a student. After proper ceremony, he launches on his own and earns his livelihood—in the prescribed manner only. Continues to be a celibate till such time as he gets married.

17. *Vivaha:* On the advice of his teacher, the boy finds himself a bride from an approved family, and is married according to the rules and regulations of the Jain religion. The couple spends seven days visiting sacred places and only then may cohabit, in the ovulation period alone, for the sole purpose of reproduction.

18. *Varnalabha:* The son leaves his father's home for the first time. The father endows part of his property to the son in the presence of witnesses and for the first

time the son sets up his own home for the purpose of leading a good and devout life.

19. *Kulacharya:* All the duties of a good householder are to be carried on faithfully.

20. *Grhisita:* Through the development of wisdom, character, etc., the layman is expected to strive to excel.

21. *Prasanti:* By delegating authority to the sons, peace and quietness should be secured.

22. *Grhatyaga:* At the attainment of ripe old age, hand over all property to the sons, advise the eldest son to carry on the family tradition, and depart for a pilgrimage.

23. *Dikshadya:* After leaving home take up duties of a pre-ascetic.

24. *Jinarupata:* Discard all robes and become an ascetic.

25. *Maunadhyayanavrtti:* Complete concentration upon one subject only.

26. *Tirthakrbhavana:* Constant reflection upon a Tirthankara.

27. *Gurusthanabhyupagama:* After due qualification, become a teacher of other ascetics.

28. *Ganopagrahana:* Through word and deed, defend the members of the Jain community.

29. *Svagurusthanavapti:* Delegate duties to disciples, become an Acharya, i.e., leader of the ascetics.

30. *Nihsangatvatmabhavana:* Devote more of his time to meditation.

31. *Yoganirvanasamprapti:* Through extreme asceticism realize the nature of the self.

32. *Yoganirvanasadhana:* Discard food and care of

the body; concentrate.

33. *Indropapada:* After death becomes an Indra, i.e., king of the gods, by virtue of his merits.

34. *Indrabhikesha:* Concecrated by the gods as an Indra.

35. *Vidhidana:* Ascends the throne of Indra.

36. *Sukhodaya:* Enjoys happiness in heaven.

37. *Indratyaga:* The pleasures of heaven are abandoned.

38. *Avatara:* He incarnates on earth into a Tirthankara.

39. *Hiranyajamata:* The soul enters the womb of a woman ready to give birth to a Tirthankara.

40. *Mandarendrabhisheka:* Indra worships him on the Meru Mountain upon his birth.

41. *Gurupujana:* Indra worships the Tirthankara designate while he is a child.

42. *Yauvarajya:* He becomes an heir apparent to the throne while in his youth.

43. *Svarajya* (literally, "self rule") : Rules over his own kingdom.

44. *Chakralabha:* He acquires the chakra, that is, the nine stores and the fourteen jewels.

45. *Digvijaya:* He commences the conquest of the universe.

46. *Chakraabhisheka:* His conquest is celebrated.

47. *Samarajya:* He guides the nobles in their duties toward their subjects.

48. *Yogasammadha:* He secures the power through austerities as well as through his omniscience.

49. *Arhantya:* He becomes an Arhat.

50. *Vihara:* The Arhat or the Tirthankara preaches the truth to all people.

51. *Yogatyaga:* Then he draws the soul unto itself. (Denies itself?)

52. *Agranirvrti:* Achieves complete and final liberation.[11]

The *Adi Purana* from which the above is quoted date back to the ninth century A.D. The Svetambaras have slight variations in their ceremonial practices, and minor variations also exist from province to province. On the whole, the ceremonies are similar to those of the Hindus.

THE LANGUAGE AND LITERATURE OF THE JAINS

The Jain community is scattered throughout India. Like "the Muslims, Sikhs and other minority community members, the Jains always use the language of the region." [12] In Poona, where Marathi is the regional language, Jains speak fluent Marathi; in the Gujrath area, as a rule, they speak Gujrathi. The founder of the sect, Mahavira, spoke Ardhamagadhi, the language in which a considerable amount of Jain sacred literature is written. Wherever they have settled, the Jains have enriched the literature of the region. A highly developed body of Jain literature exists in Hindi, Gujrathi, and Kannda. It is contended by Altekar that Jain literature did not flourish in Maharashtra (where Marathi is the lingua franca) before the tenth century because of the absence of the Jains from the area.[13]

Jain literature also abounds in the Tamil and the Telugu

languages, that is, in the southern Indian as well as the northern Indian languages. A Jainologist, B. A. Saletore, states:

> One of the best claims of Jainism at the hands of posterity is
> that it contributed to the literature of all the three provinces.
> The Jaina teachers as the intellectual custodians of the
> Andhradesha, the Tamil land, and Karmataka most assid-
> ously cultivated the vernaculars of the people, and wrote in
> them great works of abiding value to the country. Purism
> was the keynote of their compositions, although almost all
> the early Jaina writers were profound Sanskrit scholars.
> With them originated some of the most renowned classics
> in Tamil, Telugu and Kannada. It has been rightly opined
> that the Jainas gave to the Tamil people their didactic
> classics like the Kural and the Naladiyara, major and minor
> Kavyas, and quite a number of other works as well. To the
> Andhradesha and Karnataka, among other precious gifts,
> the Jains gave the Champu Kavyas or poems in a variety
> of composite meters interspersed with paragraphs in prose.[14]

Many Jain manuscripts written by Jain religious leaders in
the Acharyas, Sanskrit, Prakrit, and Apabramsa languages
still await translation into modern Indian languages. Sangave
observes that along with religion and ethics, the Jain literature
deals with such subjects as grammar, prosody, glossary,
mathematics, medicine, and astrology. Much of it deals with
the history of ancient India.[15]

JAIN HOME LIFE

At home the Jains are required to follow the principle of
ahimsa even in matters of dress. They are not permitted to
wear anything made of fur or feathers obtained as a result
of torturing animals or birds.[16] Similarly, no silk or woolen

garments are to be worn.[17] The use of leather is also restricted. Leather goods are used solely for ornamental purposes. Tiger skin, deer skin, and substitutes for leather are used whenever possible.[18]

No special clothes are worn by the Jains, with the exception that their clothes must not reveal the body contour so as to excite sexual passions.[19] They must not be extravagant in dress at any time. While the Jains have no particular ornaments, they wear more precious ornaments than members of other religious sects. Sangave states:

> The Jains are a comparatively rich community and as they deal in gold, jewels and precious stones, they put on various kinds of ornaments. Like other women, Jaina women also are more fond of ornaments than men. In ancient Jaina literature fourteen kinds of ornaments are mentioned.[20]

The dietary laws of the Jains are very elaborate. The principle of ahimsa rules out meat and fish; wine or any other liquor is also forbidden. No food may be eaten that might contain small insects or have been infested by worms. For this reason Jains are forbidden the eating of kandamulas, that is, underground stems and potatoes, garlic, radish, turnip, carrot, beetroot, or similar vegetables. Nor are they to eat figs; pipal (fruits) are the birthplace of mobile beings. Jains are very careful about eating their meals during the day since himsa (the opposite of ahimsa) is almost unavoidable if food is prepared after sunset when there is little light. Those who find it impossible to do so, observe these restrictions at least during chaturmasa, the four months during the monsoon season when insects are rife. Extreme precautions are taken to wipe all the dishes carefully so as to prevent any living creature from being injured. Similarly the Jains take great care in straining water, milk, juice, or any other liquid that is to be consumed. When a Jain travels and wishes to drink water, he covers his mouth with cloth, stoops down to a stream, and drinks by suction.[21]

Wine is believed to breed microorganisms, and is also considered to make an individual forget piety which, in turn, may cause him to commit himsa without hesitation. Wine is also forbidden because it may arouse sexual desire, anger, or pride. Because some trick may be used to obtain a honeycomb —it may be prodded loose and fall upon some living creature —honey is forbidden. Even stale butter is forbidden since, while fermenting, it may breed living creatures.[22]

Originally the Jains were very broad-minded: they disapproved of strict caste restrictions and their rules of commensalism were quite liberal. For example, the Jains originally had no objection to eating meals in the company of non-Jains, but since coming under the influence of the Hindus, they now restrict inter-dining. Sangave states that when caste feasts are given, members of other castes are generally not invited. Still, they are liberal in their social relations and have no objections to touching a so-called member of a low caste. This, Sangave asserts, is probably due to the fact that a majority of the Jains consider themselves to be Vaisyas; there are practically no Shudras among Jains.[23]

Rules of Connubium

Among the Jains, the bride is always given as a gift to the bridegroom. In the absence of the father, the rules specifically state that the girl should be given in marriage by the grandfather, brother, uncle, a person of the same gotra (literally, "herd," like the Latin "gens"; a group descended from a common ancestor, usually a legendary saint), paternal grand-father, or the maternal uncle. Only in rare cases is the girl permitted to chose her own partner. Valavakar asserts that this is permitted only in cases of extreme trouble.[24]

The bridegroom is very carefully chosen. He must be of a particular caste, free from any disease, of desirable age, educated, wealthy, from a proper family, and of good moral character. The bride likewise must be of the same caste, but of a different gotra, possess beautiful features and good health. She must be younger than the bridegroom, and from a large family. Not only the bride, but the bridegroom too is expected to be chaste before marriage. In ancient times, it was believed that the progeny of a couple where the girl was sixteen years old and the boy was twenty-five was bound to be very strong.

A father is expected to find a suitable match for his daughter when she reaches the proper age for marriage. According to the ancient belief, he who did not do so when the daughter attained puberty was sure to go to hell. In the early days of the Jain community, individuals chose their partners freely. Marriages took place frequently between Jains and non-Jains, between Aryans and non-Aryans. Gradually as the caste became rigid in the majority group, the Jains found themselves drawn along until eventually they limited marriages to those who professed Jainism. Later, as castes were formed within the Jain community, endogamy came to be the general rule rather than the exception.

The Jain scriptures state that marriage may be dissolved if the couple finds any defect in one another within a prescribed time; such a marriage is declared to be null and void. The husband is permitted to remarry if the wife is unfaithful or

neglects her household duties. The wife is permitted to remarry under the following circumstances: if a husband becomes a sinner, an ascetic, turns out to be impotent, or dies
or is presumed to be dead.[25] At present, divorce is discouraged
and the divorced woman is permitted to marry only among
very few Jain castes.

The Position of Jain Women

In ancient times, the Jain woman was comparatively free,
much less secluded than her descendants in the Ganges Valley.
Except on rare occasions her authority in the home over the
children and the Dravidian servants was not subject to restraint by her husband, although he was the acknowledged
master of the household.[26] In the *Upanishads,* Kshatriya men
as well as women are dramatized as taking part in the discussions as readily and ably as among the Brahmans.[27] However,
in later times (from the sixth century B.C. on), the position
of the woman deteriorated. In the *Laws of Manu* or the *Code
of Manu,* a metrical work of 2,685 verses, c. 500 B.C., that
deals with custom, law, religion and politics, the principle
followed by the men up to almost the present time reads:

> In childhood a female must be subject to her father, in youth
> to her husband, when her lord is dead to her sons; a woman
> must never be independent. . . . A Husband must be con-
> stantly worshipped as a god by a faithful wife. . . . [Once
> he is dead she must not marry again and] never even men-
> tion the name of another man . . . [learn to have patience,
> be chaste and strive to fulfill] that most excellent duty which
> is prescribed for wives who have one husband only. . . .
> [The widow] who, from a desire to have offspring, violates
> her duty to her deceased husband, brings on herself disgrace
> in this world . . . [such an one will fail to join her hus-

band in the next world and] will enter the womb of a
jackal.[28]

However, the *Laws of Manu* do have some favorable things
to say about women:

> Where the women are honoured, there the gods are pleased;
> but where they are not honoured, no sacred rite yields re-
> wards. Hence men who seek [their own] welfare, should
> always honour women on holidays and festivals with [gifts
> of] ornaments, clothes, and [dainty] food.[29]

On the whole, however, the *Laws of Manu* as well as texts in
the *Padmapurana* point to the superiority of the male. No
Brahman may eat in the company of his wife, nor look at
her while she eats or while she dresses. The woman's god is
her husband, whom she must seek to please all the days of
her life. On the death of her husband the Brahman wife
was expected to burn herself alive on the funeral pyre.[30]

The Jain position on the status of women is far from
liberal compared with the traditional position in Indian
society. Parsvanatha, the twenty-third Jain saviour, remarked
about the thoughts of a woman: "The wise ones know how
much sand there is in the Ganges, and how much water in
the ocean, they know the dimensions of a great mountain—
but the thoughts of a woman they cannot fathom." [31]

The Jain teacher Acharya Amitagati states the Jain point
of view in these words:

> [The female body being full of impurity, therefore is] the
> treasury of all sufferings, the bolt barring the city of heaven,
> the path of the dwelling of hell . . . the axe for the
> pleasant grove of piety, the hoar-frost for the lotus of
> virtues, the root of the tree of sins, the soil for the creeper
> of deceit.[32]

Sangave feels that the position more acceptable to the Jains is that stated by Acharya Somadeva, who felt that women are neither good nor bad; they are "like the cream of milk, the source of poison as well as nectar," and "have neither any innate merit nor blemish, but become like their husbands, as rivers assume the character of the ocean in which they merge themselves." [33] Further, Sangave comments that remarks such as "Striyo hi vismam Visham" [34] ("Women are the worst of poisons") are made in order to advise the ascetics to avoid the company of women, and as a precautionary measure, called Rajraksha (i.e., for the protection of the kings lest they be deceived by wicked women). [35]

Opinion has been divided among the Jain scholars upon the status of women. At least some of the Jain teachers have permitted women to join the ranks of ascetics along with the men. According to the *Kalpa Sutra,* three thousand female ascetics (sadhvis), joined an order under the leadership of Neminantha, the twenty-second Tirthankara, during the period of Parsvanatha (the predecessor of Mahavira), and were emancipated and found moksha. [36] Male and female members both were compelled to beg and lead a strict monastic life. [37] It was the nuns who were placed under the more rigorous routine and forbidden to study the chapters of *Mahaparijna, Arunopapata* and the *Drshtivada* because of the magical formulas contained in the *Drshtivada* which were supposed to be somewhat dangerous for women, since they were regarded as fickle-minded. [38] Additionally, nuns were allowed to ask for alms only when led by an experienced monk.

Female infanticide cannot possibly occur in the Jain community because it violated the principle of ahimsa, or noninjury to any living creature. Excellent provisions are made for the maintenance of unmarried women, who, by Jain law, are accorded an allowance from the family income.[39]

The institutions of the family, church, school, and state have served as agencies for the spread of education among the Jain women in India. A Jain girl is expected to be proficient in sixty-four arts including dancing, painting, music, medicine, and domestic science. Throughout their history Jain women have chosen to enter the teaching profession as it enables them to remain unmarried and free to develop spiritually.[40] Female education declined when child marriage was introduced around 300 B.C. Today, male literacy is five times that of the female in the Jain community.

Because of the principle of ahimsa, not only infanticide but the dreadful Hindu practice of throwing the widow on the funeral pyre of the husband (sutee) was absent from the Jain community. Unlike Hindu widows, those of the Jains were never tonsured, and only very rarely have they adopted the custom of wearing purdah, a veil, while visiting friends or relatives. The Jain widows have fared better than their Hindu counterparts and have engaged themselves in many tasks at home.[41]

The widow, according to Jain law, automatically acquires the property left by her husband. Being at the mercy of the mother, the son therefore behaves himself. This, Sangave believes, is one reason why the rates of juvenile delinquency are so low among the Jains.[42]

JAIN CHARITABLE INSTITUTIONS

Jain charitable institutions are not limited to the Jain community alone: some exist for the benefit of the community at large.[43] Jains are very tolerant of other religions and open their charitable institutions to all, irrespective of caste or creed. Every layman is expected to give some gift to others. The gifts are of four kinds: ahara-dana (food); abhaya-dana (protection); aushadha-dana (medicine); and sastra-dana (learning). Keeping this in view, the Jains in their own way have contributed in all four fields.

In every large town or place of pilgrimage, Jains have opened dharmasalas (rest houses) where the weary traveler may refresh himself. These are provided with simple amenities such as bedding and utensils. Most are free with occasional exceptions where a nominal fee is charged. In the province of Gujrath alone, there are 266 rest houses belonging to the Svetambara sect.[44]

Sangave observes that beast as well as man is welcome to this protection. Animal rest houses are known as panjarpolas. Lame, useless, and aged animals are sent to the panjarpolas and often these animals are purchased by the Jains in order to save them from their inevitable fate at the hands of the butcher. In Gujrath there are sixty-five panjarpolas.[45] Some are exclusively for the insects which are collected carefully from the streets and fed gently.

Human suffering is alleviated through dispensaries and hospitals. Here little or no charge is made for medicine and treatment. In a majority of the cases the treatment is ayurvedic.[46]

There is some evidence that in ancient times medicine and food, as well as education, were furnished in the Jain mathas (religious halls).[47] Today the Jains give very generously to education, either building educational institutions completely with Jain funds or contributing large sums to already existing public institutions. The Jains have also contributed generously to famine-stricken areas.[48] Sangave observes that there is no humanitarian cause which does not get sympathetic help from the Jains.[49]

Jain institutions of a purely religious character include Jain libraries called grantha-bhandaras (literally, "treasure house of books"). These are indeed treasure houses, in that they usually contain well-preserved ancient manuscripts written on parchment or palm leaves, in addition to printed books. Wherever there are Jains, libraries abound. In Gujrath alone there are fifty-six grantha-bhandaras.[50]

Despite the existence of a vast amount of literature pertaining to Jain history, it has been available for translation and study only in recent times. As early as the beginning of this century, the Jains were opposed to putting into print any of their sacred books from the grantha-bhandaras. Today, the policy is to make this literature available freely, and many institutions have been established to circulate the books.[51]

Apart from publishing religious books, there are institutions called pathasalas (religious schools). The Digambaras and the Svetambaras have their separate pathasalas. Learned men instruct the Jain laymen in religious doctrines, etc. In ancient times institutions known as bhattarakas existed in many places; today some can still be found in Gwalior, Jaipur, Nagpur, Kolhapur, Hyderabad in the Mysore district, and in Kanchi. Bhattarakas were founded to encourage the Jain laymen to continue in the faith in spite of the surrounding Muslim rulers who frowned upon the Jain practice of nudity.

Lastly, there are institutions which are of a social nature and have the welfare of the Jain community exclusively in mind. Associations such as the Bombay Yuvaka Sangha, a youth organization, and Bharata Jaina Mahamandala, a general organization, are examples of institutions which cater solely to the Jains. There are also Jain newspapers and journals. Finally, there are cooperative societies for helping Jains provide themselves with better housing at reasonable prices. These are sectarian, and membership is restricted to caste members.

SUMMARY

The set of principles that guide the Jains in their daily conduct are specifically related to their religious doctrines. In the eyes of non-Jains, their form of worship, their religious philosophy, and the strict ascetic conduct of both monks and laymen are very peculiar. Rules of conduct are inevitably designed to achieve the main religious aim, moksha. This is true not only for monks but also for laymen, for whom the rules are as precise as for the monks: they touch on every department of life.

The Jains are pluralists believing that there are many gods and goddesses, none superior to any human being. The objects of contemplation are the Tirthankaras who have already achieved nirvana. The life of the Jain layman is regulated by various ceremonies through which he passes from his cradle to his grave, each step having as its sole objective the achievement of moksha.

The Jains are scattered throughout India where they have adopted the regional languages and enriched the literature wherever they have settled. A large proportion of this literature deals with the history of ancient India as well as a variety of subjects including religion and ethics, grammar, prosody, mathematics, medicine, and astrology.

At home the Jains are required to follow the principle of ahimsa even in matters of dress. Wearing furs or feathers is forbidden and the use of leather is severely restricted. Conservative styles are favored though clothing usually follows the style of the region. Jain women are permitted to wear ornaments and since many Jains are merchants, gold and silver are readily available. Dietary laws are very elaborate: meat, fish, and wine or other liquors are forbidden in accordance with ahimsa, as are potatoes, onions, garlic, radishes, carrots, beetroot or any vegetable which may contain a multitude of small insects. All liquids must be strained or filtered. Since it is difficult to avoid himsa at night, meals may be eaten only during the day and then only in the fellowship of acceptable members of the community.

Marriages are arranged by the elders and can be dissolved within a prescribed period. Men are invariably permitted to remarry; the remarriage of women is permitted under certain circumstances. The Jain woman, on the whole, has fared well in spite of the traditional Indian belief that woman is the root of all evil. Some of the Jain women have been permitted to join the ranks of the ascetics. Neither female infanticide nor the practice of sutee were ever practiced among the Jains. Many Jain women have entered the teaching profession which has permitted them to remain single and to grow spiritually. The widow, according to the Jain law, automatically acquires all property left by her deceased husband.

Jain charitable institutions are open to both the Jain and non-Jain. Every layman is expected to contribute something toward the betterment of his neighbor. Many hospitals have been opened by the Jains; their schools and colleges have helped hundreds to obtain education. Jain institutions, of a purely religious character, include libraries, religious schools, newspapers, journals, and cooperative societies with the specific purpose of helping to solve the housing problem.

NOTES

1. Vilas Adinath Sangave, *Jaina Community, A Social Survey* (Bombay, 1959), p. 211.

2. Philippians 2:12–13.

3. Sangave, *Jaina Community*, p. 237.

4. Mrs. Sinclair Stevenson, *Notes on Modern Jainism* (Surat, 1910), p. 94.

5. H. V. Glassenap, *Der Jainismus* (1897), as quoted by Sangave in *Jaina Community*, p. 238.

6. Sangave, *Jaina Community*, p. 237.

7. Ibid., p. 245.

8. Ibid., p. 258

9. Ibid.

10. Due to early marriages, puberty sometimes was attained after the girl had been married for some years.

11. *Adi Purana*, 38:55–62 and 70–312. See Sangave, *Jaina Community*, pp. 259 ff.

12. Sangave, *Jaina Community*, p. 283.

13. A. S. Altekar, *Rashtrakutas and Their Times* (Poona, 1934), pp. 412–13.

14. B. A. Saletore, *Medieval Jainism* (Bombay, 1938), pp. 262–63.

15. Sangave, *Jaina Community*, p. 286.

16. C. R. Jain, *Jain Culture* (Bijnore, 1934), p. 47.

17. C. Krause, *Heritage of the Last Arhat* (Bhavnagar, 1930), p. 9.

18. Sangave, *Jaina Community*, p. 282. Frequently, very wealthy Jains in India are found wearing canvas tennis shoes for this reason.

19. Jain, *Jain Culture,* p. 49.

20. Sangave, *Jaina Community,* p. 283.

21. Ibid., pp. 279–80.

22. Ibid., p. 281.

23. Ibid., p. 82. One reason why the surrounding culture could not influence the Jains too greatly was possibly the nature of their occupations. The Jains, being mostly merchants, had to have social intercourse with people of all castes: it was simply good business policy to serve the customer without respect to color, caste, or creed. Possibly this is the same reason why some of the businessmen in the southern part of the United States do not object to serving Negroes.

24. Ibid., p. 147.

25. Ibid., p. 173.

26. John B. Noss, *Man's Religions* (New York, 1956), p. 116.

27. Ibid., p. 128.

28. G. Buhler, trans., "The Laws of Manu," in *Sacred Books of the East,* ed. F. Max Müller (Oxford, 1896), 25:195, v. 148; 196, vv. 154, 157, 158; 197, vv. 161, 164.

29. Sarvepalli Radhakrishnan and Charles A. Moore, *A Source Book in Indian Philosophy* (Princeton, N. J., 1957), pp. 189–90.

30. Noss, *Man's Religions,* p. 227–28. In many orthodox families the wife prostrates herself each morning. A distinguished philosopher who served as a visiting lecturer in the United States about ten years ago was rudely awakened by the contrast in the position of women in America. He vowed that upon his return, he would eat with his wife and, for the first time in many years of married life, make sure that there would always be enough food for *both* of them. He was amazed that with all his scholarship, he had not learned the importance of being more careful in these matters. Of course, India is changing and women are gradually claiming equality with men.

31. M. Winternitz, *History of Indian Literature* (Calcutta, 1933), 2:575.

32. Ibid., pp. 562–63.

33. Sangave, *Jaina Community,* p. 179.

34. Acharya Gunabhadra, "Atmanusasana," in *The Sacred Books of the Jainas,* ed. J. L. Jaini (1928), 7:135, 129–31. Cited by Sangave, *Jaina Community,* p. 179.

35. K. K. Handiqui, *Yasastilaka and Indian Culture* (Sholapur, 1949), p. 106. Cited by Sangave, *Jaina Community,* p. 179.

36. Hermann Jacobi, "The Kalpa Sutra," in *Sacred Books of the East,* ed. F. Max Müller (Oxford, 1896):22, 7.

37. M. A. Indra, *Status of Women in Ancient India* (Lahore, 1940), p. 303.

38. A. S. Altekar, *Position of Woman in Hindu Civilization* (Benaras, 1938), p. 247.

39. C. R. Jain, *Jain Law* (Madras, 1926), pp. 95, 130.

40. D. C. Dasagupta, *Jain System of Education* (Calcutta, 1942), p. 58. Cf. "The unmarried woman careth for the things of the Lord, that she may be holy both in body and in spirit: But she that is married careth for the things of the world, how she may please her husband." I Corinthians 7:34.

41. Sangave, *Jaina Community,* pp. 184, 188.

42. Ibid., pp. 192–93.

43. Evidence of the proverbial nature of Jain charity in ancient India is given by the following ancient story.

> After Visakha, Migara's mother, had been roused, rejoiced, gladdened, delighted by the Lord with talk on Dhamma, she asked him to consent to accept a meal from her on the morrow together with the Order of monks. The Lord consented by becoming silent. Then towards the end of that night heavy rain poured over the "continents." . . .
>
> When the time for the meal had come, Visakha sent a servant woman to the monastery to announce the time. She saw the monks, their robes laid aside, letting their bodies get wet with rain, but she thought they were Naked Ascetics [i.e., the Ajivikas, an important sect contemporary with Buddha, not monks]. . . . When Visakha had served and satisfied the Order of monks with the Buddha at its head with sumptuous food, solid and soft, she sat down at a respectful distance, and spoke thus to the Lord:

"Lord, I ask for eight boons from the Lord."

"Visakha, Tathagatas are beyond granting boons."

"Lord, they are allowable and blameless."

"Speak on, Visakha."

"I, Lord, for life want to give to the Order clothes for the rains, food for those coming in [to monasteries], food for those going out, food for the sick, food for those who nurse them, medicine for the sick, a constant supply of conjey [porridge], and bathing cloths for the Order of nuns."

"But, having what special reason in mind do you, Visakha, ask the Tathagata for the eight boons?"

"Lord, my servant woman told me there were no monks in the monastery, but Naked Ascetics were letting their bodies get wet with the rain. Impure, Lord, is nakedness, it is objectionable. It is for this special reason that for life I want to give the Order cloths for the rains.

"And again, an in-coming monk, not accustomed to the roads or resorts for alms, still walks for alms when he is tired. But if he eats my food for those coming in, then when he is accustomed to the roads and resorts for alms he will walk for alms without getting tired.

"And again, an out-going monk, while looking about for food for himself, might get left behind by the caravan, or, setting out tired on a journey, might arrive at the wrong time [the wrong time for eating is after noon until sunrise the next day] at the habitation where he wants to go. But if he eats my food for those going out, these things will not happen to him. . . . And, again, Lord, if an ill monk does not obtain suitable medicines, either his disease will get very much worse or he will pass away. But this will not happen if he can use my medicine for the sick." . . .

"It is very good that you, Visakha, are asking these eight boons." Then the Lord, on this occasion, having given reasoned talk, addressed the monks, saying: "I allow, monks, cloths for the rains, food for those coming in, medicine

for the sick, a constant supply of conjey, bathing-cloths
for the Order of nuns."

From Edward Conze, ed., with I. B. Horner, D. Snellgrove,
A. Wiley, *Buddhist Texts Through the Ages* (Oxford, 1953),
pp. 26, 28.

44. *Jaina Svetambara Directory,* 1, 2:522.

45. Ibid.

46. Sangave, *Jaina Community,* pp. 287–88. Ayurvedic is the
ancient system of Indian medicine, handed down from the first
century A.D. Through contact with the Greeks, the development
of medicine was considerably enhanced. An increased use of mer-
curial drugs along with opium and sarsaparilla is found after the
influence of the Arabs. Most medical ideas were similar to those
held by the early medieval Europeans. Bone setting was done with
some skill and plastic surgery was performed better than anywhere else. The East India Company surgeons consulted the
Indian surgeons. Because of the taboo against contact with dead
bodies, the progress of physiology and biology was impeded.
The doctrine of ahimsa encouraged the development of veterinary
practice. See A. L. Basham, *The Wonder That Was India* (New
York, 1954), pp. 499–500.

47. *Journal of the Bombay Branch of the Royal Asiatic Society*
(Bombay, 1841), 1, 2:522. Cf. the Jewish Synagogue which
served as a place of communal assembly since it was the focus of
Jewish religious, social, and intellectual life as well as elementary
school, law court, and even hostelry for strangers.

48. M. B. Jhavery, *Historical Facts about Jainism* (Bombay,
1925), pp. 17–18.

49. Sangave, *Jaina Community,* p. 288. Frequently the Jains
are accused of being humanitarian for selfish reasons. It is felt that
were it not for religious motives they would not indulge in such
large-scale charities. The motive may often be questioned but never
the fact that they are a very charitable people.

50. *Jaina Svetambara Directory,* p. 523.

51. Sangave, *Jaina Community,* p. 289.

7

ECONOMIC
ETHIC OF
THE JAINS

The Jains believed that severest asceticism was essential to purge contaminating matter from one's soul and to save it from all evil. Maintaining the purity and integrity of one's soul also demanded the ceaseless practice of noninjury to any and all living beings (ahimsa). This pursuit of asceticism had a far-reaching effect on the Jain community.

Though the Jain laity was not expected to follow the rigorous routine laid down for the monks, lay persons were held under disciplinary control by means of routine inspections by the clergy and the guardians of morality.[1] Literally every department of the individual's life was affected.

The monks naturally devoted their lives to religious vocations. But for laity in a predominantly agricultural country the choice of vocations was limited. Since no work could be undertaken which involved even the possibility of the destruction of any living creature, one could not be a butcher, fisherman, distiller of liquor or manufacturer of ammunition.

Jain scriptures list the following as being undesirable activities for a Jain in view of the vow of ahimsa: castrating an animal, clearing of trees or plants, drying up lakes or rivers, or any activity where an unusual use of fire is involved.[2]

While the founders of Jainism were mostly Kshatriyas, the present-day Jains are Vaisyas (the merchant caste). They are called Baniyas or Vaniyas.[3] Many Jains prefer to regard themselves as outside of and distinct from the Hindus and their caste system. Most Jain authorities are agreed that the Jains are predominantly engaged in business. Sangave states:

> The Jainas follow practically all sorts of avocations but they are mainly money-lenders, bankers, jewellers, cloth merchants, grocers and recently industrialists. As they hold the key positions in all three occupations, it is no wonder that a large proportion of mercantile wealth of India passes through their hands.[4]

Basham comments:

> But though the history of Jainism is less interesting than that of Buddhism, and though it was never so important, it survived in the land of its birth, where it still has some two million adherents, mostly well-to-do merchants.[5]

The Jains have been living in India for more than two millennia: they could not possibly have survived as traders only.

When Jainism became the official state religion in some kingdoms, an accommodation to worldly demands had to occur. Some adjustment had to be found with respect to military service, just as it did in ancient Christianity. As the doctrine of the king and the warriors was revised, violation of ahimsa was possible "in wars of defense." The ancient prescription was now reinterpreted to mean that for the laity it precluded only the killing of "weaker" beings, that is un-armed beings.[6]

However, the Jains took the doctrine of ahimsa very seriously, occasionally paying a very heavy price in order to be true to their faith. It is said that the consequences of these ritual prescriptions—for instance, a Jain may never go through water lest he step on insects—contributed to the downfall of Jainism. The Jainistic king, Komarpal of Anihilvara, lost his throne and life because he would not permit his army to march during the rainy season.[7]

In time the practice of ahmisa led to the virtual exclusion of the Jains from all industrial trades endangering life: trades that made use of fire, involved work with sharp instruments (wood or stone), masonry, and, in general, the majority of industrial callings. Agriculture was, of course, completely excluded: ploughing, especially, always endangers the lives of worms and insects.[8]

Besides ahimsa, the laity was expected to limit its possessions. Personal effects were to be restricted to necessities. Possession of riches beyond those necessary for existence was considered detrimental to spiritual growth. Surpluses should be given to the temple or to the protection and care of animals. This in turn would earn merit for the devout, generous Jain. As Jainism later developed, the acquisition per se of considerable wealth was in no way forbidden, but only the striving after wealth and attachment to riches. Weber compares this with the Protestant idea that "joy in possessions" (parigraha) is objectionable, not possessions or gain in itself. A Jain commandment forbids saying anything false or exaggerated; hence the Jains believed in practicing absolute honesty in business. All deception (maya, "illusion") was prohibited, including, especially, all dishonest gain through smuggling, bribery, and any sort of disreputable financial practice.[9]

If one was not permitted to take bribes, it hardly made it worthwhile for a Jain to enter such professions as government service where the forms of "political capitalism" permitted one to accumulate wealth by serving as a tax collector or a state surveyor. Not only was the honesty of the Jain trader famous, but the wealth accumulated by the Jains became proverbial.[10]

The Svetambara Jains, upon whom the restrictions placed were far more rigorous, became mainly traders. A trader could practice ahimsa more easily than a nontrader. The religious laws demanding that Jains restrict their travel for ritualistic reasons encouraged them to settle in resident trade. This influenced the Jains, like the Jews, to take up banking and money-lending. Weber states:

> The compulsory "saving" of asceticism familiar from the economic history of Puritanism worked also among them toward the use of accumulated possessions, as investment capital rather than as funds for consumption or rent. That they remained confined to commercial capitalism and failed to create an industrial organization was again due to their ritualistically determined exclusion from industry and as with the Jews their ritualistic isolation in general.[11]

Similarities with the Puritans in the strict methodical nature of their prescribed way of life proved very helpful to the Jains in accumulating wealth. Abstinence from intoxicants, meat, and honey, avoidance of all unchastity, loyalty in marriage, and avoidance of status pride and anger regulated the daily life of a Jain. He simply had no way left in which to squander his wealth. At the same time, the warning against naive surrender "to the world"—to avoid entanglement in karma through rigid, methodical self-control and composure, through holding one's tongue, and studious caution in all life situations—helped the Jain to further accumulate wealth.[12]

The institutions and doctrines of most present-day communities have changed over the centuries. However, Jainologist Sangave asserts that such is not the case with the Jain community. In fact, he states the important reason for the survival of the Jain community is its inflexibile conservatism in holding fast to its original institutions and doctrines for the last centuries. Sangave says:

> The most important doctrines of the Jaina religion have remained practically unaltered up to this day and, although a number of the less vital rules concerning the life and practices of monks and laymen may have fallen into disuse or oblivion, there is no doubt that the religious life of the Jaina community is now substantially the same as it was two thousand years ago. This strict adherence to religious prescriptions will also be evident from Jaina architecture and especially from Jaina sculpture, for the style of Jaina images has remained the same to such an extent that the Jaina images differing in age by a thousand years are almost indistinguishable in style. Thus an absolute refusal to admit changes has been considered as the strongest safeguard of the Jainas.[13]

ECONOMIC LIFE IN ANCIENT INDIA

The belief that ancient Indian society was not an acquisitive one is not based on facts as revealed in most early Indian literature. The Brahman priest who was supposedly given

over to the ideals of austerity and spiritual growth, often
amassed considerable wealth doing service of a religious nature. He officiated at the sacrifices and performed marriages
and other domestic services.

Many Brahman landowners have lived in great wealth.
Poverty was considered to be living death. In the *Rig Veda*
many prayers are found which contain wishes for obtaining
wealth. While ascetics undoubtedly were highly honored,
Basham observes:

> The ideas of ancient India, while not perhaps the same as
> those of the acquisitive West, by no means excluded money-
> making. India had not only a class of luxury-loving and
> pleasure-seeking dilettanti, but also one of wealth-seeking
> merchants and prosperous craftsmen, who though less re-
> spected than the Brahmans and warriors, were honoured in
> society.[14]

Mention is made of private producers who manufactured
on a large scale for a wide market. According to an early
Jain text, a wealthy potter named Saddalaputta owned five
hundred potters' workshops, had a fleet of boats, and distributed his wares throughout the Ganges Valley.[15]

A money economy existed in India only since the time of
Buddha. It was probably borrowed from the West, possibly
from Persia. The earliest coins consisted of flat pieces of
silver or bronze in irregular shapes, but fairly accurate in
weight. Though there is no evidence of a highly organized
financial system of checks, drafts, and letters of credit—usury
was widespread, and money-lending, except by Brahmans,
did not incur the reprobation of Hindu moralists, as it did
that of the medieval priests of Christianity and Islam.[16] The
Rig Veda and the *Dharma Sutras* both mention indebtedness.

In the latter, rates of interest are also mentioned, as are regulations governing debts and mortgages. Rates vary from 1.5
percent a month to 15 percent a year. There is a sliding scale
of interest prescribed for unsecured loans, according to the
class of the debtor: Brahmans 24 percent, Kshatriyas 36 percent, Vaisyas 48 percent, and Sudras 60 percent a year.
Kautilya's *Arthshastra* mentions short term loans as 5 percent
per month; interest paid by merchants traveling through for-
ests was 10 percent; and seafaring merchants were obliged to
pay 20 percent. Basham asserts that these enormous rates of
interest—60, 120, and 240 percent per year respectively—are
the measures of both the profit and the risk of ancient Indian
commerce.[17]

The shreshti [18] combined the role of merchant with that
of the moneylender or banker. Banking traditionally has been
carried on in India by the merchants who amassed immense
wealth.[19] A class of large merchants, as distinct from small
traders and pedlars, existed at least from the time of the
Buddha. The Jataka stories speak of shreshtis cornering grain
and buying at their own price the products of craftsmen who
were virtually at their mercy. The term *shreshti* was a title of
honor reserved for merchants of wealth and consequence.
Buddhist scriptures mention shreshtis being honored by kings.
Under the Gupta rulers the chief banker or shreshti was sometimes a member of the advisory council.[20]

The Jains became successful merchants, bankers, and
moneylenders. Basham remarks that:

> Jainism encouraged the commerical virtues of honesty and
> frugality, and at a very early period the Jaina lay com-
> munity became predominately mercantile. The splendid
> Jaina temples at such places as Mount Abu and Sravana

Belgola are testimonies of the great wealth and piety of
medieval Jaina laymen.[21]

It is entirely possible that the existence of Kautilya's
Arthasastra helped indirectly at least the merchants and the
traders. *Arthasastra,* originally written with the express purpose of helping the king in his political and economic affairs,
contained many valuable ideas which could be utilized by anyone interested in running his own business enterprise in a
profitable manner. It contained counsel on the importance
of increasing one's wealth: "Wealth, virtue, and enjoyment
form the aggregate of the three kinds of wealth. Of these, it
is better to secure that which is mentioned first than that
which is subsequently mentioned in order of enumeration." [22]

Kautilya did not consider trade or manufacture to be in-
ferior to agriculture. The merchant was indeed honored and
guarded against theft. Lending money or material at interest
or for profit was not condemned, although it was subject to
regulation in that limits were put on the amounts to be
repaid and maximum rates were prescribed for various types
of loans.[23]

Jagdhish Chandra Jain, an authority on the Jains in ancient
India, observes that the material documenting the economic
conditions in India is too fragmentary to present a systematic
account of the economic life of the people in ancient India.[24]

The *Jatakas,*[25] a collection of stories included in the
Khudaka-Nikaya of the *Suttapitaka* of the Pali canon, are considered by many authorities as a very important source of
knowledge of the period between Mahavira and Buddha.
Rhys Davids remarks:

> The popularity of the *Jatakas* as amusing stories may pass
> away. How can it stand against the rival claim of the fairy

tales of Science and the entrancing, many sided story of man's gradual rise and progress? But though these less fabulous and more attractive stories shall increasingly engage the attention of ourselves and of our children, we may still turn with appreciation to the ancient book of the Buddhist *Jataka* tales as a priceless record of the childhood of our race.[26]

In ancient India the rulers depended upon taxation and other sources for the support of the state. The *Vyavahara Bhasya* mentions that one-sixth of the produce was collected as legal tax, which was regulated according to the produce, the cost of cultivation, the condition of the market, and the nature of the soil. According to Jain legend, a merchant who had twenty vessels gave one as a royal tax.[27] Next to the land revenue, commerce was the largest source of revenue for the rulers.[28]

THE NATURE OF WEALTH

During the period of the *Jatakas,* wealth consisted of gold, silver, precious metals, oxen, horses, cattle, fields and stores of grain (kotthagara), slaves, and hired laborers. The organization of industry was based on the private ownership of property, land and the means of production and distribution. A considerable number of occupations became hereditary about this time.

Ratilal Mehta asserts that a money economy had already come into existence.[29] Maganlal A. Buch observes that the treasurer general, who was the custodian of the public treasury, used to receive coins into the treasury, carefully distinguishing between the genuine and the counterfeit ones. The treasurer general who was in charge of grains, merchandise, raw materials, and weapons of the royal storehouse "shall have so thorough a knowledge of both internal and external incomes running even for a hundred years that, when questioned, he can point out without hesitation the exact amount of net balance that remains after expenditure has been met out." [30]

Department of Accounts

Buch observes that in ancient India, the details of revenue collection were placed on record. Among the details entered into the books were the number of the various departments; the description of the work in each department; the amount of profit, loss, expenditure, and delayed earnings; the number of operations; the wages paid; the values of precious gems on hand; and payment of provisions, lands, and tribute from or to friendly or inimical governments. A general report on the financial position of the state was submitted by the superintendents to the members of the cabinet each month. [31]

The mercantile classes had to be very careful in their dealings with the rulers, as well as in those with the public at large. If a merchant raised the price of a commodity owing to competition, the extra money earned was confiscated by the king. Fabrications of accounts were severely punished. Merchants who dealt in gold, silver, diamonds, precious stones, horses, and elephants paid a higher rate of taxes than artisans and those who dealt in grains and bronze. [32]

Capital

Mehta observes that in ancient India only a minority of people possessed capital: the rich tradesmen—the Setthis or in some cases the rich Brahmanas.[33] Rich tradesmen were called the dhanavantas (literally, "very wealthy"). At times they possessed untold amounts of silver, gems, pearls, corals, and jewels inherited from their fathers.[34]

MERCHANT ORGANIZATIONS

Important craftsmen such as goldsmiths and painters were organized into guilds called seni. Jain texts, as well as those of the Buddhists, mention some eighteen guilds.[35] The seni was organized in the form of a union with a view to promote the welfare of its members.[36] Frequently mentioned tradesmen (vanija) possessed no membership in any organization. Trade passed through the hands of middlemen who were vanija or resident traders.[37]

The often-mentioned Setthi in the *Jataka* stories was, according to Fick, the German Buddhist scholar, not only a head of some class of industry but probably a representative of the commercial community.[38] He appears to have had a double role, namely that of official and of rich trader. He was expected to obtain the formal permission of the king when the ruler wished to renounce the world or give his wealth away to charity. He was more influential as a merchant prince than as an official.[39]

Jain nuns as well as monks were supported by the merchants. Occasionally, this relationship was abused by merchants who were lay Jains; under the pretext of giving alms, some householders, in rare cases, raped the nuns. If a nun became pregnant under such unfortunate circumstances, she was to be under the care of the sravaka;[40] however, if the circumstances were known publicly she was kept in the

Upasraya and was not sent out for alms. A story is told of a
Buddhist merchant of Bharuyaccha who took the garb of a
Jain layman and invited nuns aboard his ship under the
pretext of offering them alms; once on board he set the ship
in motion.[41]

NOTES

1. Max Weber, *The Religion of India,* trans. Hans H. Gerth
and Don Martindale (Glencoe, Ill., 1958), pp. 202 ff.

2. S. C. Rampuria, *Cult of Ahimsa* (Calcutta, 1947), p. 22.
It should be noted that this does not mean that a butcher or
a person involved in the manufacture of liquor cannot be a Jain.
Nor does it mean that no Jain is permitted to work as an agri-
culturist or be in the armed forces. The first Tirthankara permitted agriculture as well as service in the army. However, this was
eventually regarded as permissible only as a matter of expediency.
Today a person who takes up such a profession (and there are
some in the state of Karnataka who till the land for a living)
can be a Jain, but he will be in the vowless stage of soul evolution
and, since every Jain is concerned with the salvation of his soul,
he will engage in this type of activity only as a last resort. In
Gujrath there are a few Jains who are agriculturists; some have
entered the armed forces. See J. L. Jaini, *Outlines of Jainism*
(Cambridge, England, 1916), p. 72.

3. Here is an occurrence of a shift in class position. The
doctrines of Jainism forced the majority of Jains to give up the
more prestigious Kshatriya caste. Kshatriyas were the warriors
and there were even Jains who served as generals in the army.
When ahimsa forced them to take up professions in keeping with
Jain regulations, most became traders, merchants, and indus-
trialists. In the hierarchy of the caste system it was permissible

to move down but extremely difficult to move up the ladder; one could not start, for instance, being a Sanskrit scholar and learning the Hindu scriptures, calling oneself a Brahman priest, unless one was actually born a Brahman. The Jains in their quest for moksha were prepared to be called Vaisyas rather than remain Kshatriyas. Cf. "What shall it profit a man if he gain the whole world and lose his own soul?" (Mark 8:36). Kshatriyas could be merchants and traders but the break was so radical that they were referred to eventually by others as Vaisyas and the name stuck.

4. Vilas Adinath Sangave, *Jaina Community* (Bombay, 1959), p. 279.

5. A. L. Basham, *The Wonder That Was India* (New York, 1954), p. 287.

6. Weber, *The Religion of India,* p. 199.

7. Ibid., p. 365.

8. Ibid., p. 199. In the case of the Digambara sect, the monks practice rigorous asceticism; however, they do not make rigorous demands upon the laity, and those Jains who did work in agricultural occupations were usually Digambaras rather than Svetambaras. Some of the agriculturists, realizing that their Jain brethren who had migrated to the cities and become traders were doing far better economically, followed their example. This has happened again in recent times. Sangave mentions that Cutchi Visa Osavalas, finding that occupation in agriculture could not support large families in their native village, migrated to Bombay City. Sangave, *Jaina Community,* p. 346.

9. Weber, *The Religion of India,* p. 200. This was tempered to mean that if the truth is unpleasant, silence is to be observed. One should not deliberately deceive. It was believed that a Jain who practiced deception would be born a woman in the next life, something most undesirable. Cf. the Quaker practice of remaining silent and not giving any helpful information regarding prices, etc., to other competitors.

10. Ibid.

11. Ibid.

12. Ibid., p. 201.

13. Sangave, *Jaina Community,* p. 399. See also Jarl Charpentier, *Cambridge History of India* (Cambridge, 1922) 1:169, and V. A. Smith, *History of Fine Art in India and Ceylon* (Oxford, 1911), p. 267.

14. Basham, *The Wonder That Was India,* p. 216.

15. Hoernle, ed., *Uvasaga Dasao* (Calcutta, 1899), 1:105. Cited by Basham, *The Wonder That Was India,* p. 216. Buddhist India was by no means a pure agricultural country, but had much industry and manufacturing. Commerce, manufacturing, and agriculture were the chief sources of wealth. Regular trade on a large scale occurred between the great cities of the kingdom. Since the city itself was not convenient for the many merchants who visited from afar in their caravans, market towns grew up near each city. Merchants took five-hundred cartloads of merchandise to their trading centers or cities. The horse dealers brought their horses from the North; the merchants from Kasi brought their cloth; and Benares sent her famous muslins and other manufactured products. From A. P. de Zoysa, *Indian Culture in the Days of the Buddha* (Columbo, 1955), pp. 130, 134.

Within the country, produce was brought to market for sale. Benares was one of the most important commercial centers. The other large cities also commanded a considerable amount of trade and exchange.

Foodstuffs for the towns were brought to the gates, apparently from the villages, and sale transactions were carried on there. There were apanas (shops) where commodities were displayed for sale. Merchants could enter into partnership or temporary partnership. However, disputes often arose as to the sharing of profits. The commodities sold in these apanas were textile fabrics, groceries and oil, green vegetables, grain, perfumes and flowers, articles of gold and jewelry, carriages, arrows, etc. The hawkers carried their wares for sale in portable trays.

"Prices were not fixed and there was competition by which dealers wanted to prevail upon the purchasers. . . . The vice of adulteration was not unknown. On the part of the buyers there was the haggling of price." From Bimala Churn Law, *India as*

Described in Early Texts of Buddhism and Jainism (London, 1941), pp. 188–91.

16. Basham, *The Wonder That Was India,* p. 221. Coins appear to have been the chief medium of exchange, but the more primitive medium of barter was not unknown, though not as usually practiced. In the *Jatakas* almost all kinds of prices, fees, pensions, fines, loans, and incomes have usually been stated in terms of coins of different denominations.

Besides actual currency there were several other legal instruments of exchange. Mention is made of letters of credit by means of which big merchants in large cities obtained money from fellow merchants. There is also mention of promissory notes. See Law, *India as Described in Early Texts,* pp. 188–91.

17. Basham, *The Wonder That Was India,* p. 221. There were no banks, and banking facilities were few; however, loans could be obtained. Money-lending was looked upon as an honest calling, "but this had already given to profit-mongering." Money was lent against bonds (panna); however there were instances of bad debts which were never repaid. Money-lending was done by professionals while ordinary people hoarded their wealth and concealed it underground or deposited it with friends. The nature and amount of such hoarded wealth was recorded on gold or copper plates. See Law, *India as Described in Early Texts,* p. 191.

18. The word *shreshti* means "chief." In Pali it is *setthi.* Today the variation *sheth* is the name frequently used for the leading merchants and particularly Jain merchants. The Jain *Who's Who* almost invariably carries the title Sheth before the name; for instance we read of Sheth Kasturbhai Lalabhai, Sheth Ambalal Sarabhai, Sheth Walchand Hirachand, Sheth Kantilal Ishwardas, Sheth Punamchand Ghasilal, Sheth Shanti Prasad Jain of Dalmia, Sheth Sir Shantidas Ashukaran, and Sheth Sir Chunilal B. Mehta.

19. Maganlal Buch states that trade was a regular profession and gives an illustration of how a merchant rose from small beginnings to ultimate fortune: Once when Bodhisatta was a treasurer in Benares and on his way to wait upon the king, he

came on a dead mouse lying on the road. Taking note of the position of the stars at that moment, he said: "Any decent fellow with his wits about him has only to pick that mouse up, and he might start a business and keep a wife." A young man picked up the mouse, which he sold for a farthing to a tavern-keeper for his cat. With the farthing he bought molasses, and then took drinking water in a waterpot. Coming upon flower gatherers returning from the forest, he gave each a tiny quantity of molasses and ladled the water out to them. Each in turn gave him a handful of flowers, with the proceeds of which he returned the next day to the flower grounds provided with more molasses and a larger pot of water. That day the flower-gatherers gave him flowering plants with half their remaining flowers; and in a short while he had obtained eight pennies.

Later on, one rainy and windy day, the wind blew down a quantity of rotten branches and the gardener could not see how to clear them away. Up came the young man with an offer to remove the lot, if the wood and leaves might be his. The gardener accepted the offer on the spot. Just then the king's potter, on the lookout for fuel, came upon this heap which he bought for sixteen pennies, as well as five bowls and other utensils. Having now twenty-four pennies in all, a plan occurred to him. He went to the city gate with a jar full of water, and supplied five hundred mowers with water to drink; and as he went about, he struck up an acquaintance with a land-trader, and a sea-trader. Said the former to him: "Tomorrow a horse-dealer is coming with five hundred horses to sell." On hearing this piece of news, he said to the mowers: "I want each of you today to give me a bundle of grass, and not to sell your own grass till mine is sold." Unable to find grass for his horses elsewhere, the dealer purchased our friend's grass for a thousand pieces of coin.

A few days later his sea-trader friend brought him news of the arrival of a large ship and another plan struck him. He hired a carriage and went in great style down to the port. He then bought the ship on credit, depositing his signet ring as security, and had a pavilion pitched close by. To his pupil as he took his seat inside he said: "When the merchants are being shown in, let

them be passed on by three successive ushers into my presence."
Hearing that a ship had arrived in port, about a hundred merchants came down to purchase wares, only to be told that there
were none to be bought as a great merchant had already made
a payment on account. They all proceeded to the young man, and
the footmen duly announced them by three successive ushers.
Each merchant gave him a thousand pieces to buy a share in the
ship, and then a thousand to buy him out altogether. In this way
he earned 200,000 pieces. The treasurer, on hearing the story,
gave him his own daughter and on the old man's death the youth
became treasurer in the city. Maganlal A. Buch, *Economic Life in
Ancient India* (Baroda, 1924), 2:340–343.

20. Ibid., p. 222.

21. Ibid., p. 293.

22. Arthsastra 9, p. 7, Cited by Ralph Braibanti and Joseph
Spengler in *Administration and Economic Development* (Durham,
N. C., 1963), p. 240.

23. Ibid., p. 254. Also the availability of a system of nine digits
and a zero with place notation for the tens and hundreds (from
about 594 A.D.), and the use of the decimal system which the
Arabs themselves have called "the Indian (art [Hindisat])," in all
probability aided the development of a rational accounting system
and provided a great boon to the merchants in keeping their
records. See Basham, *The Wonder That Was India,* pp. 495–96.

24. Jagdish Chandra Jain, *Life in Ancient India as Depicted
in the Jain Canons* (Bombay, 1947), p. 87.

25. V. Fousboll, ed., *Jataka,* trans. and ed. E. B. Cowell (Cambridge, England, 1895–1913).

26. Rhys Davids, *Buddhist Birth Stories* (London, 1917), pp.
136–137.

27. According to Buddhist scriptures, the method of taxation
was to levy taxes without causing hardships. "In this way the
taxes on the people are light, and the personal service of them
is moderate. Each one keeps his own worldly goods in peace,
and all till the ground for their subsistence. Those who cultivate
the royal estates pay a sixth part of the produce as tribute. The
merchants who engage in commerce come and go in carrying

out their transactions. The river passages and the road barriers are open on payment of a small toll. When the public works require it, labour is exacted but paid for. The payment is in strict proportion to the work done." *The Buddhist Records of the Western World,* bk. 2, cited by de Zoysa in *Indian Culture in the Days of the Buddha* (Columbo, 1955), p. 134.

28. Jain, *Life in Ancient India,* p. 61.

29. Ratilal N. Mehta, *Pre-Buddhist India* (Bombay, 1939), p. 182.

30. Buch, *Economic Life in Ancient India* (Baroda, 1924), 2:342.

31. Ibid., pp. 342–343.

32. Ibid., p. 361.

33. Mehta, *Pre-Buddhist India,* p. 211.

34. Jain, *Life in Ancient India,* p. 108.

35. Commerce was not accomplished through mere individual efforts. At one time, the collective enterprise of eighteen guilds appeared in one city. Skilled workers such as mariners, garland-makers, caravan traders, masons, blacksmiths, carpenters, painters, etc., belonged to these eighteen guilds. In another city, a rich man was described as having done "good service both to the King and to the Merchants' guild." Rich merchants of the cities had already formed themselves into a class which was made up of "members of merchant families." de Zoysa, *Indian Culture in the Days of the Buddha,* p. 134.

36. Jain, *Life in Ancient India,* p. 109.

37. Mehta, *Pre-Buddhist India,* p. 231.

38. Richard Fick, *The Social Organization in North-East India in Buddha's Time* (Calcutta, 1920), pp. 259 ff.

39. Mehta, *Pre-Buddhist India,* p. 219.

40. Sravaka is an order of lay Jains who were merchants prosperous enough to be able to support an order of monks and nuns who specialized in doing good works in the community. Cf. Quakers.

41. Jain, *Life in Ancient India,* p. 167.

PART FOUR

COMPARISON
AND CONCLUSION

8

COMPARISONS
AND CONTRASTS

To pinpoint the many similarities that appear between the Quakers and the Jains—as well as their differences—it would help us to compare the two groups at this point.

SOCIAL MILIEU

The social milieu in which Quakerism arose in the West and Jainism in the East are, obviously, quite distinct. Quakerism is comparatively recent, having originated in the early seventeenth century; Jainism began as early as 500 B.C. George Fox was surrounded by the influence of the Judeo-Christian dualistic philosophy of the West; Mahavira found himself in the midst of the monistic philosophy of the East.

The society in which Mahavira was born already had a strongly developed class hierarchy in which a common dharma (a general norm of conduct which all had to follow) was recognized, as well as a dharma appropriate to each class and to each stage of the individual's life. The dharma of men of high birth differed from that of the lower class; similarly, the dharma of a student was not that of an old man.[1] Fox in England found himself in a society where the class structure was not so fixed. Ritual fraternization existed between classes, as depicted in the Lord's Supper commensalism; the king and the pauper could theoretically come together as equals.

Fox, uneducated and from a poor family, had nothing to lose by challenging the powers of his time. Had Mahavira not been born a Kshatriya, he could not have exercised the immense influence he did upon the people of his day. Had he been born an untouchable, it is almost certain that his influence would have been negligible.

All early kings in India claimed to be descendants of a god or a goddess. The Buddhist and the Jains had the audacity to reject the king's godhead. Fox, too, found it difficult to reconcile the king's claim to divine right with the brutalities of warfare associated with the professed religious aims and zeal of the Puritans.

PACIFISM AND AHIMSA

Fox denounced the devil as being the author of all wars and strife. All who pretended to fight for Christ were deceived, since the kingdom of Christ is of heaven and not of earth. A Quaker youth, if he could not accept this principle, could expect no further guidance from the Quaker group. Military service during the early period of Quakerism was considered an offense; it was an almost unpardonable sin for a true Quaker to take up arms. Quakers have never compromised on the issue of war and peace.

The first of the five great vows of Jainism is ahimsa, non-injury to any living thing, a principle the Jain not only practiced but exhorted others to follow. The doctrine of ahimsa, carried to the point of not eating any meat, fish, or vegetables grown underground, was responsible for Jainism's pacifistic ideas, for they were a natural extension of the principle of noninjury.

Many conscientious objectors are found among the Quakers; similarly, very few among the Jains have joined the armed forces.

HIGH LEVEL OF PIETISM

Because of their religious beliefs, the Quakers were often treated as an outcast minority community. The separatist and semi-ascetic attitude toward those outside the group was reinforced by loyalty to the group. The Quakers formed a model sect. A good Quaker was drawn by the Inner Light, which guided each individual, into close fellowship with those who were like-minded. The Quaker meeting was concerned with the details of daily life of each Quaker. Their "queries" or questions were often centered upon such mundane items as the clothing the members wore.

No Quaker wished to hide his identity. Through his peculiar style of life, he made known to the world that he was a member of the Quaker group. The meeting was very like a confessional. The individual placed before the members all his activities and sought guidance for the future. Since no Quaker could afford to be disowned by the Meeting House, he was always prepared to be disciplined by the group.

The Jains, also a minority community, regulated not only

the life of the monk with various ceremonies, but also the life
of Jain laymen by religious principles intended to prepare
them for the final liberation, moksha, the ultimate aim of an
individual's life.

The counterpart of the Quaker Meeting House was the
Upasraya—the lecture hall. Through the Upasraya, the Jain
layman was taught what was expected of him in daily conduct,
including his business practices. Because he was concerned
with the problem of ultimate liberation and was anxious to
have the guidance of the elders in the community, no Jain
could afford to ignore the Upasraya. This served as a confessional for the Jain layman.

MIGRATION TOWARD THE CITIES

The Quakers migrated to the cities, abandoning their agricultural pursuits. The frequently large and rapid profits of
trade, compared with the small and slow returns from agriculture, may in part have induced this change from an agrar-
ian to an urban community. Because of their refusal to take
oaths, the Quakers could not hold public offices requiring an
oath prior to appointment. Freedom for activity was found
in the areas of commerce, medicine, and law, which could be
carried on better in the cities than in the rural areas.

The seriousness with which the Jains practiced ahimsa soon
led to their virtual exclusion from all industrial trades that
endangered life. Agriculture was, of course, completely excluded; ploughing, especially, always endangers the lives of
worms and insects. Nor could a Jain afford to accept bribes
because of religious prohibitions; without bribes there was
little inducement to enter a profession such as government

service. This refusal to accept bribes had a similar affect on the Jains as did the Quakers' inability to take oaths. For the Jain as for the Quaker, migrating to the city with its possibilities for trade seemed the most natural course to take. The Jains still flock to the Indian cities where they can engage in commercial activities without compromising the doctrine of ahimsa.

BUSINESS ETHICS

Honesty in business was expected of every Quaker; at meetings he had to give a detailed account of his dealings. The Quaker businessman had religious reasons for being both efficient and honest. His fame spread abroad and soon non-Quakers began trading with the Quakers because they could be certain of an honest deal. There was some truth in the accusation that the Quakers kept trade within their own fold. By corresponding with other Quaker merchants, the Quakers shared information about trade opportunities and reinforced their fellowship with other Quakers. Quaker merchants were extremely cautious and prudent, meticulously accurate in details, and insistent that others be so. They acquired a reputation for driving hard bargains. Through sobriety, industry, and honesty they became wealthy.

The Jains, who migrated to the cities and became traders, also became well known for their honesty. A Jain commandment forbids saying anything false or exaggerated and the Jains applied this principle to business. All deception was prohibited—especially dishonesty through smuggling, bribery, and any disreputable financial practices. Jains, too, developed a close relationship with other Jain merchants. This was to be expected as they shared a common meeting place, the Upasraya, the counterpart of the Quaker Meeting House. Their reputation for honesty in business inevitably drew the trade of non-Jains.

ASCETICISM

The Quaker was encouraged to detach himself inwardly from the world. Quakers were taught in the meetings to "empty" themselves, surrender themselves, deny themselves, and outwardly engage themselves in activities. This was described as "obeying Him whose service is true liberty." Simplicity in all things was practiced by the Quakers. This simplicity was a reaction to dogmatism, royal prerogative, and worldly extravagance. Education shied from impractical, artistic subjects, emphasizing instead pragmatic learning to gain an honest livelihood.

Asceticism was considered essential both by the Jain monks and the laymen. The monks took the five great vows: (1) ahimsa (noninjury to any living thing); (2) astya tyaga (against untruthfulness); (3) asteya vrata (nonstealing); (4) brahmacarya vrata (chastity); and (5) aparigraha vrata (renouncing all love for anything or any person). Jain laymen were exhorted to develop serious demeanor, cleanliness, good temper, moderation, caution, gratitude, humility, and attention to business.[2]

SOCIAL PROBLEMS

Quakers find religion to be most compelling when it is reduced to its simplest terms—the love of God and one's neighbor. They have never followed a policy of isolation, but rather have been deeply concerned for their fellow man. In whatever the Quakers undertook, they expressed the desire to create humane and dignified conditions of living—even for the man who had no property—as the first prerequisite of morality and religious life.[3] There was no line of demarcation between those who carried on social service and those who engaged exclusively in nonsocial work activities. Every Quaker is expected to face up to his social responsibilities.[4] From the earliest days of the movement, Quakers have taken an active part in poor relief, education, rehabilitating alcoholics, public health, care of the insane, prison reform, and the abolition of slave trade and slavery. The principle of self-help rather than charity was observed. Proverbial Quaker wealth was never haphazardly donated to charity; rather, the same rational procedures were used to make the best use of the money available as were used to accumulate it. In the Meeting House, the Quakers deliberated and organized the precise manner and nature of the help to be given.

The Jain monks constantly regulated the lives of the Jain laymen through the supervision of the Upasraya. The monk was engaged in religious work and could not spare time to engage in any commercial activity. Still, he had to be supported, and this the Jain layman undertook as a holy duty. The Jain layman could hardly squander his wealth for he, too, was occupied with the thought of doing everything possible to achieve liberation and this precluded any relaxation of ascetic practices. Part of the wealth was diverted toward the support of the monks; alms-giving was considered a sacred duty. Many a Jain layman has made philanthropic gestures expecting to receive spiritual merit in return. This has resulted in the establishment of hospitals, rest houses, educational institutions, and homes for animals that are aged and disabled, expressing the Jain principle of reverence for all living things.

SUMMARY

Despite the distinctly different social milieu of Jainism and Quakerism, the sects have many similarities. Both were pacifistic in nature: Quaker pacificism finds its counterpart in the Jain doctrine of ahimsa. Both Quakers and Jains have religious gatherings of a confessional type. Both sects were reluctant to enter government service for religious reasons. Their business activities were regulated by the Meeting House of the Quakers and the Upasraya of the Jains. Their policy of being honest at all times in business established for each sound business reputations. The non-Quakers preferred to trade with Quaker merchants and non-Jains with Jain merchants. Trade misrepresentations were scrupulously avoided. Both groups accumulated wealth that could not be squandered. Social work was given prominence by both the Quakers and the Jains. The Quakers, who believed that all men were equal and that they were their brother's keeper, channeled a considerable amount of their energies to alleviate human suffering. Because alms-giving was considered helpful, the Jains also channeled their wealth in a philanthropic way, securing merit toward liberation. Finally, both the Quakers and the Jains migrated to the cities. The Quakers did so because economic opportunities were greater; the Jains, because they could not engage in agricultural and allied occupations where the life of any living thing was endangered.

NOTES

1. A. L. Basham, *The Wonder That Was India* (New York, 1954), p. 137.

2. Don Martindale, *Social Life and Cultural Change* (New York, 1962), p. 197.

3. August Jorns, *The Quakers as Pioneers in Social Work,* trans. Thomas Kite Brown (London and New York, 1931), p. 98.

4. According to Rev. Harold N. Tollefson, minister of the Friend's Church, Minneapolis, Minn., it is not unusual for two business partners to take turns at doing social work. While one partner looks diligently after the business, the other engages himself fully in social work.

9

SUMMARY AND
CONCLUSION

We began with a brief discussion of Max Weber's study of the emergence of the psychology of capitalism in the West, in *The Protestant Ethic and the Spirit of Capitalism.* Weber conceived capitalism with its pursuit of profit by means of continuous, rational, capitalistic enterprise to be peculiar to the West. Various elements of capitalism have appeared outside the West in many places and forms: capitalistic acquisition, with the rational pursuit of profits resting on calculations in terms of capital; the conduct of business activity in terms of a balanced ascertainment of profit and loss; the capitalistic entrepreneur. Weber also observed that only in the West was rational industrial organization attuned to a regular market, rational bookkeeping and legal separation of corporate and personal property, and the integration of science into the service of the industrial organization.[1] Weber theorized that essential elements of the psychology, which he has termed the "spirit" of capitalism, were produced by Puritan worldly asceticism.

The present study was motivated by Weber's famous study. The cross-cultural comparison of two groups,—the Quakers and the Jains—was carried out to examine the interrelations of economic behavior and religious ethics under extremely different social conditions. Do Jainism and Quakerism have similar economic consequences as a product of somewhat similar religio-ethical principles even in the face of radically divergent social surroundings? This is the question we have tried to answer.

RELIGIOUS AFFILIATION
AND SOCIAL STRATIFICATION

Weber states that national and religious minorities often prefer to enter business life because they are excluded from political office or the service of the state. This was not true, however, of the Catholics in Germany who shunned the business life of the community. Weber theorized that the ascetic characteristic of the Calvinistic churches was an essential element in the industrial and capitalistic development of the Puritans. This observation formed the basis for choosing the Quakers and the Jains for a cross-cultural study.

The Quakers and the Jains both stress ascetic discipline in everyday deportment, and both have developed an unusual business acumen. This suggests that there is a connection between their religious ways of life and the intensive development of business ability among sects whose other-worldliness is as proverbial as their wealth, in spite of their different social contexts.[2]

THE SPIRIT OF CAPITALISM

At the time of its rise, capitalism was associated with a special psychology which turned economic activity into a religious duty. It is "the idea of a duty of the individual toward the increase of his capital, which is assumed as an end in itself." [3] Success in business was taken as a measure of religious worth. At the same time, success was no excuse to relax, but served instead to elicit greater efficiency. Such a psychology promoted the capital accumulation required by early capitalism.

The Quakers, in a manner typical of the Protestant sects, were interested in succeeding in business as an end in itself, that is, as an example and proof of religious worthiness. No amount of prosperity was grounds for self-satisfaction and, as no Quaker could afford to be disowned by the Meeting House, he continued to process profits into the enterprise and to carry on his business in a diligent, honest, and prudent manner.

The Jain laity was constantly under the supervision of the monks in a manner paralleling the supervision of the Quaker by the meeting. In their daily conduct, lay Jains were expected to follow the rules laid down for them by the monks. It was the holy duty of the Jain laity to carry on their daily business activities and to succeed in their ventures.

In the Upasraya, where the Jains had to account for their daily activities, wise counsel was given to those who needed it. The Jain merchant, like his Quaker counterpart, desired to accumulate money, not for what it would buy, but as an end in itself, or as evidence of his piety. Accumulating wealth was a goal that assured the Jain he was progressing toward his ultimate goal, namely, liberation. For both the Quaker and the Jain, earned wealth brought primarily the psychological satisfaction that a job had been done well.

CONCEPT OF THE CALLING

In Protestant circles, the concept of calling summarized a sense of the life-task that, though involving everyday worldly activity, had religious significance. "The only way of living acceptably to God was not to surpass worldly morality in monastic asceticism, but solely through the fulfillment of the obligations imposed upon the individual by his position in the world." [4]

The Quakers accepted this philosophy wholeheartedly. They felt no need of the monastic life in order to serve God; their obligations could be fulfilled in everyday worldly activities. Some Jains, indeed, gave themselves over totally to the monastic way of life. However, the laity was expected to regard its daily activity with a sense of religious significance, as preparation for eternal liberation.

Neither the Quakers nor the Jains retained a traditionalistic concept of calling such as Luther held. In Luther's conception, since everyone was waiting for the coming of the Lord, there was nothing to do but simply remain in the worldly occupation in which the Lord had placed one. [5] The Quakers and the Jains pursued a more activistic notion of individual calling. They were prepared to change their station in life and did so deliberately in order to be more effective in their worldly activity. This they did for the glory of God and for salvation. Instead of passively submitting to their lot, they rationally ordered the course of their lives.

THE INFLUENCE OF CALVINISM

The pious man of the Reformation was occupied with one thing—his eternal salvation. This preoccupation was an entirely individual matter. No priest or sacrament could help him. Each believer asked himself the questions: Am I one of the elect? And how can I be sure of this state of grace? Although it was held an absolute duty to consider oneself chosen and to combat doubts as temptations of the devil, to attain this mighty self-assurance in individuals engaged in intense worldly activity. It helped dissolve religious doubts and gave the certainty of grace.[6] While the Calvinist was not able to achieve salvation alone, at least worldly success helped him in his conviction of it. Good works did not secure salvation, but they were necessary as a sign of election—they were an outward sign of the inward conviction. Moreover, the God of Calvinism demanded of His believers not single good works, but a life of good works combined into a unified system.[7]

Since the life of the saint was directed solely toward salvation, it was thoroughly rationalized with the aim of bringing glory to God on earth.[8] The Occidental monastic life, unlike that of the Orient, was of a rational nature. The monk was trained objectively as a worker in the service of God; and this rationality was carried over into the practical daily life of the lay individual. The Reformation Christian had to be, in effect, a monk all his life. The ascetic ideal had to be pursued within mundane occupations. "By founding its ethic in the doctrine of predestination, it substituted for the spiritual aristocracy of the predestined saints of God within the world."[9] Calvinism, with its doctrine of predestination, thus methodically rationalized ethical conduct.

Historically the Quakers belong to the Puritan movement. Early in his experience, George Fox discovered that only Christ could speak to the heart. The inward experience of realizing the consciousness of Christ became the most fundamental tenet of Quakerism. With the aid of the Inner Light, every Quaker felt his own spiritual pulse. The importance of the sacraments was belittled. Charles M. Woodman states that "in its place they attempted to live the sacrament in their relations with their fellow men." All life and all human conduct was a sacrament. No higher ideal for human action had ever been set.[10]

The Quakers have a positive belief in eternal life. Through rediscovery of moral and spiritual grandeur, faith in immortality was reinforced. Each step of the way the individual was expected to walk according to the light within him; therefore the Quaker was encouraged to be inwardly detached from the world. Simple dress became an honorary badge of membership in the group—a testimony to distinguish oneself from the rest of the world. Ascetic ideals channeled their energies in their daily conduct.

The Calvinists maintained the necessity of proving one's faith in worldly activity. Similarly, the Quakers, by laboring diligently in their chosen calling, expected the Lord to bestow His blessing in the form of material prosperity. Business success was regarded as a sign that the Lord was indeed guiding them with the Inward Light. From childhood they were taught to order their tasks, their thoughts, and every moment of their lives. These virtues were not accidental but deliberately cultivated.

Like the man of the Reformation, the Jain was occupied with the question of eternal salvation. The life of the Jain layman was regulated by various ceremonies through which he passed from the time of his birth to the time of his death. "The ceremonies are prescribed by religion with a view that a layman would lead a life in accordance with the religious principles and attain the main aim of final liberation." [11] Severe asceticism was considered essential to preserve one's soul from evil. Maintaining the purity and integrity of one's soul involved the practice of noninjury. Since the Jain laity was not expected to follow the rigorous routine of the monks, it was kept under disciplinary supervision.

Laymen, in keeping with the ascetic proscription, limited their personal possessions. Though the acquisition of wealth was in no way forbidden, the striving after wealth and the attachment to riches was. Like other Oriental monks, Jain monks devoted their whole lives to spiritual activities, taking time off to discipline the life of the Jain laymen. They recognized the importance of bringing order to those who carried on mundane activities. With the doctrine of ahimsa before them, they tried to methodically rationalize the ethical conduct of the Jain layman.

Sacraments were of little or no importance. Not even God could help the Jain achieve liberation. Mahavira declared to his disciples: "Man thou art thine own best friend, why seekest thou another?"

ASCETICISM AND
THE SPIRIT OF CAPITALISM

English Puritanism, which derived from Calvinism, exemplifies the consistent religious basis for the idea of the calling.

Richard Baxter wrote extensively on Puritan ethics; Spener on German Pietism; Barclay on Quakerism.

Baxter considered wealth a great danger, for its temptations seemed never-ending. Asceticism, for Baxter, seems to have turned much more sharply against the acquisition of earthly goods than it did for Calvin, who saw no reason to hinder the accumulation of wealth by the clergy: he expected them to use it profitably.[12]

One must never relax in the security of one's possessions. Not leisure and enjoyment, but activity alone adds to the glory of God. Time must never be wasted; rest is for Sundays only. Baxter stressed the value of hard work not only in one's calling, but throughout the range of life's activities. Unwillingness to work was considered symptomatic of the lack of grace. Baxter allowed no exceptions. Even the wealthy were expected to work, since all had a calling in the providence of God. Any accomplishment outside of one's calling was of minor significance. In the Puritan concept of calling, the emphasis was always on the methodical character of worldly asceticism, in contrast to Luther who expected man to be satisfied with his lot.[13] If one of the elect had a chance to profit, it was his duty to take advantage of the opportunity. God may not require that one always labor to be rich. So long as wealth does not encourage idleness and sinful enjoyment, it was the duty of the individual to acquire it.

The ascetic interpretation of calling provided ethical justification for the modern specialized division of labor. It also justified the profit-making activities of the businessman. It held in esteem the sober, middle-class, self-made man. "God blessed his trade," was a common remark of the time.

Since idle talk, expensive clothing, and vain ostentation

were indications of impiety, there was a tendency toward uniformity in life, which "to-day so immensely aids the capitalistic interest in the standardization of production, had its ideal foundations in the repudiations of all idolatry of the flesh." [14] Against the glitter and feudal magnificence, which was economically unsound, developed the sober simplicity which has become the ideal of the middle-class home.

Capital accumulation through the ascetic compulsion to save served to increase the capital by freeing wealth for productive investment. Middle-class fortunes were not absorbed as they were by the feudal nobility. Even the farmer was respected if he became a rational cultivator. The bourgeois businessman could accumulate wealth and as long as his conduct was spotless and he made the proper sorts of investments, he could also enjoy the assurance that he was fulfilling his calling. "The power of religious asceticism provided him in addition with sober, conscientious, and unusually industrious workmen, who clung to their work as to a life purpose willed by God." [15] Furthermore the view of labor as a calling became accepted by the modern worker in the same way the businessman regarded his work as God's calling.

Puritans who turned Quaker did not shed their Puritanism. But the early Quakers went beyond their Puritan contemporaries. While the Quakers agreed with the high code of the Anabaptists, they rejected their monastic attitude toward the material world. By laboring diligently in one's chosen calling, Quakers fully expected the Lord to bestow His blessing in the form of material prosperity. Success in business was, indeed, a sign that the Lord was guiding them with the Inward Light. Tolles remarked that the faithful and diligent Friend, living austerely in accordance with the "Simplicity and Truth," almost inevitably accumulated wealth for "the Honour of God and Good of Mankind." [16]

No one could be idle in the calling. As early as 1741, Thomas Chalkley remarked, "The Farmer, the Tradesman, and the Merchant, . . . they must not neglect their Calling, or grow idle in their Business, but must certainly work, and be industrious in their Callings." [17] Frugality was often recommended on religious grounds as essential to that austere simplicity of life which truth demanded. However, it was justified on "practical grounds as tending to increase one's capital and credit." Quaker honesty and dependability became a by-word with non-Quakers. The Quaker ethic demanded not mere labor but specifically rational labor. Against the feudal and monarchical forces which protected the pleasure-seekers against the rising middle-class morality, Weber states that the ascetic conduct of the Quakers was carried to such an extent that as a matter of principle, even "sport was accepted if it served a rational purpose, that of recreation necessary for physical efficiency. . . . Impulsive enjoyment of life, which leads away both from work in a calling and from religion, was as such the enemy of rational asceticism." [18]

The Jains, too, followed a path of rigorous asceticism which led to a limitation in their choice of occupations. No Jain was interested in land for land's sake (as in farming). Under the disciplinary control of the monks and the principle of ahimsa, the Jain eventually became an urban dweller, usually a tradesman. Here his asceticism was, if anything, even more total than that of the Quaker. His honesty was proverbial. He worked diligently for religious reasons which drove him to seek moksha as his life's goal.

Personal effects were limited; possessions beyond the necessary ones were considered to be detrimental to spiritual growth. Surplus wealth was invested wisely or channeled toward the upkeep of temples, the support of monks, care of animals, and for the social welfare of the needy and destitute. The more one earned, the greater was the capacity to channel one's wealth in the right direction. All this contributed toward earning merit which helped the Jain layman in his attainment of moksha. Thus, there was absolutely no limit to the amount of wealth that could be acquired, as long as it was invested wisely and part of it diverted toward good works.

Like the Quakers, Jains became bankers and moneylenders, and amassed immense wealth. This too was part of the calling of the Jain layman. In reality, the Jain layman had to earn more than what was required for his own support, since it was his sacred duty to support not only himself and the members of his family, but the order of monks and various charitable institutions. This he could do only by following his calling in a systematic, rational manner. Wealth was not to be squandered, but made the most of.

SUMMARY

Despite differences in their religious practices and philosophies, the Quakers and the Jains exhibit striking similarities. Both groups are pacifistic in nature. Both for religious reasons are reluctant to enter government service. The business activities of each are regulated by the church. Both have been known for their honesty in business dealings. Both are very ascetic in their daily life. Neither group objects to increasing its wealth; in fact, both consider it their sacred duty to do so as long as it is invested wisely and the dividends diverted toward useful ends—such as educational institutions, charities, and various social reform activities. In short, they share the same quality of ethos. Basically it is the idea of individual duty toward the increase of capital which, to a degree, is an end in itself. It assumes not only commercial daring but the character of an ethically colored maxim for the conduct of life. Finally, both the Quakers and the Jains have located in urban centers.

The Quaker was interested in proving the grace of God in his chosen vocation by striving to excel in his daily activity; the Jain was interested in excelling in his chosen calling in order to attain liberation. The Quaker gave his full attention to his work under the supervision of his own Inner Light and the Meeting House. The Jain was reminded of his duty by the discipline of the monks; he could hardly relax from his calling.

Today in the land of the Jains, the development of capitalism no longer depends upon religious asceticism. Victorious capitalism, since it rests upon an industrial foundation, no longer needs the support of religion. Today the choice has vanished; one either accepts the modern economic order or perishes. However, it is valuable that the Jains, a minority community, developed most of the essentials of the spirit of modern capitalism centuries ago. The conditions were not ripe, however, for their becoming to the entire Indian social order what the Protestants became in relation to the West. Now, with capitalism entering India from the West, the Jains are unusually well equipped to play a dynamic role in the social order.

NOTES

1. Don Martindale, *The Nature and Types of Sociological Theory* (Boston, 1960), p. 384.

2. Max Weber, *The Protestant Ethic and the Spirit of Capitalism,* trans. Talcott Parsons (New York, 1958), pp. 44.

3. Ibid., p. 51.

4. Ibid., p. 80.

5. Ibid., p. 84.

6. Ibid., pp. 111, 112.

7. Ibid., p. 117.

8. Ibid., p. 118.

9. Ibid., p. 121.

10. Charles M. Woodman, *Quakers Find a Way* (Indianapolis, 1950), p. 78.

11. Vilas Adinath Sangave, *Jaina Community* (Bombay, 1959), p. 258.

12. Weber, *The Protestant Ethic,* p. 157.

13. Ibid., p. 162.

14. Ibid., p. 169.

15. Ibid., p. 177.

16. Frederick B. Tolles, *Meeting House and Counting House* (Chapel Hill, N.C., 1948), p. 57.

17. Thomas Chalkley, "A Journal or Historical Account of the Life, Travels, and Christian Experiences of that Antient, Faithful Servant of Jesus Christ," in *A Collection of the Works of Thomas Chalkley* (Philadelphia, 1749), pp. 97–98.

18. Weber, *The Protestant Ethic,* p. 167.

STATISTICAL APPENDIX
ON THE QUAKERS
AND THE JAINS

In our text we have primarily addressed ourselves to the relation between socioreligious ethic and economic conduct as illustrated by the Quakers of America and the Jains of India. Max Weber has developed the thesis that in the West the linkage of inner-worldly asceticism derived from religious norms had placed an important, though not exclusive role, in the rise of capitalism. If this were true, it opened the possibility that the Jains of India should display many of the traits of the capitalist despite the fact that he flourished in a non-capitalistic milieu. At the same time, the comparison of the Jains of India with the Quakers of the West was suggested by the fact that while their inner-worldly asceticism found a milieu more appropriate than that of the Jains to the emergence of a capitalistic psychology, the Quakers had in addition to their inner-worldly asceticism, strong pacifistic traditions that made them somewhat comparable to the Jains. As a result of these combinations the Quakers and Jains have become, so-to-speak, mirror images of one another: the Jains have preserved their capitalism, the Quakers their pacifism against the tide in their respective countries.

It is conceivable that the reader might be interested in the quantitative extent of the phenomena of Jainism and Quakerism. The following three tables make it quickly apparent that Jainism is primarily confined to India, Quakerism to the United States. Moreover the Quakers and Jains are relatively small minorities of their respective countries, which would suggest the unusual social effectiveness of their cultural components, for they have had influence on their respective societies far out of proportion of their comparative numbers.

TABLE 1

QUAKER AND JAIN POPULATIONS: 1961

GROUP	Home Country Total	World Total
Quakers	122,585 (United States)	195,519
Jains	2,127,267 (India)	*

SOURCES: Ministry of Information and Broadcasting, *India 1962* (Faridabad: Government of India Press, 1962); Walter R. Williams, *The Rich Heritage of Quakerism* (Grand Rapids, Mich.: William B. Eerdmans Publishing Co., 1962), pp. 269-270.
* Figure not available.

TABLE 2

JAIN POPULATION OF INDIA: 1961

	Population	Number of Jains	Percent of Whole
India	437,202,747	2,027,267	0.46
	States of India		
Andhra Pradesh	35,977,999	9,012	0.03
Assam	11,860,059	9,468	0.08
Bihar	46,457,042	17,598	0.04
Gujarat	20,621,283	409,754	1.99
Jammu and Kashmir	3,583,585	1,427	0.04
Kerala	16,875,199	2,967	0.02
Madhya Pradesh	32,394,375	247,927	0.77
Madras	33,650,917	28,350	0.09
Maharashtra	39,504,294	485,672	1.23
Mysore	23,547,081	174,366	0.74
Nagaland	*	*	*
Orissa	17,565,645	2,295	0.01
Punjab	20,298,151	48,754	0.24
Rajasthan	20,146,173	409,417	2.03
Uttar Pradesh	73,752,914	122,108	0.17
West Bengal	34,967,634	26,940	0.08
	Union Territories and Other Areas		
Delhi	2,644,058	29,595	1.11
Himachal Pradesh	1,348,982	95	0.01

SOURCE: Ministry of Information and Broadcasting, *India 1962* (Faridabad: Government of India Press, 1962).
* Figures not available.

TABLE 3

QUAKER POPULATION OF THE UNITED STATES
BY FRIENDS MEETINGS: 1961

Five Years Meeting		Friends General Conference	
Alaska	1,500	Baltimore	2,206
Baltimore	1,168	Illinois	933
California	8,099	Indiana	650
Indiana	13,648	New England	1,612*
Iowa	6,055	New York	3,356*
Nebraska	316	Philadelphia	17,659
New England	1,613*	Green Pastures	
New York	3,355*	Quarterly Meeting	181
North Carolina	14,649		26,597
Western	12,402	Conservative Friends	
Wilmington	4,538	Iowa	874
	67,343	North Carolina	250
		Ohio	872
		Western	50
			2,046
Independent (Orthodox)		Others	
Yearly Meetings		Pacific	2,560
Central	515	New Meetings (Monthly	
Kansas	8,302	Meetings only)	1,367
Ohio	6,721		3,927
Oregon	5,565	Grand Total	122,585
Rocky Mountain	1,569*		
	22,672		

Population of United States	Number of Quakers	Percent of Whole
180,003,175 (1960)	122,585	0.06

SOURCE: These statistics have been compiled from the available data of the Friends World Committee, Philadelphia. Walter R. Williams, *The Rich Heritage of Quakerism* (Grand Rapids, Mich.: William B. Eerdmans Publishing Co., 1962).
* These Yearly Meetings are affiliated with both the Five Years Meeting and the General Conference, so membership has been here divided equally.

GLOSSARY

Ādi-purāṇa One of the most important Jain sacred books, dating from the ninth century, which contains the sacred lore and principles of the religion.

ahiṃsā The cardinal principle of refraining from any act which might bring injury to any living thing.

ahiṃsā vrata The vow to act in accordance with the principle of noninjury. One of the five major vows for Jain monks.

ajīva All that is not (a-) the life-monad (jīva); firstly space, a comprehensive container enclosing not only the universe, but also the non-universe, and which is indestructible.

aṇu-vrata Any of the lesser vows of Jainism prescribing correct attitudes and behavior for lay persons. These are contrasted with the major vows intended for monks.

aparigraha vrata The vow to never form any (selfish) attachment to any object or person in this world. Essentially, absolute renunciation necessary for final liberation. One of the five major vows for Jain monks.

Arahat-hood   The stage of "worthiness" achieved by an enlight-
        ened person when the passions and limited interests of
        common life have been extinguished.

artha   The goal or material objects which one has successfully
        acquired in the world. Essentially, worldly motivation and
        its fruits.

Artha-śāstra   Genre of ancient Indian text describing the political
        and material objectives of life and the correct strategy
        needed for acquiring them.

Aruṇopapāta   One of the ancillary Jain sacred texts.

asatya-tyāǧa vrata   The vow to forsake all untruths in both word
        and deed. One of five major vows for Jain monks.

asteya vrata   The vow to never commit any act of theft. One of
        the five major vows for Jain monks.

āyurvedic   Pertaining to the native Indian theory and practice of
        medicine originating in the first centuries of our era
        (A.D.).

Bāṇiya   A member of the merchant class from the Jain com-
        munity of western India.

Bhairava   The Hindu deity representing the fearsome aspect of
        Shiva.

Bhaṭṭāraka   Ancient school in which the venerable monks gave
        instruction to novices in the principles of religion and
        philosophy.

Brahmā or Brahman   The single universal force which pervades
        everything which exists, according to Hindu philosophy.
        It is therefore final and impersonal reality. Often referred
        to as Brahmā-Ātman since this life force forms the soul or
        essence of all creatures.

brahmacārya vrata   The vow to lead a life of celibacy. One of the
        five major vows for Jain monks.

Brāhmaṇ or Brahmin   A member of the Hindu class of priests.

Brāhmaṇas   Ancient Hindu texts describing the ritual of sacrifice
        and its symbolic significance.

Chāndogya Upanishad   One of the principle ancient Hindu texts first preoccupied with the notions of reality and existence.

Chāturmāsa   The four-month period of the rainy season.

dharma   The moral, social, and religious behavior of each person appropriate to his class and caste.

Dharma-śāstra   Genre of ancient Hindu texts which are the authoritative descriptions of the differing expected behavior of individuals.

Digambara   One of the two principal sects of Jain monks. They received their name from the fact that they did not wear clothing. Their garment (ambara) is the element that fills the four quarters of space (dig).

Dīgha Nikāya   One of the principal texts of Buddhism which describes the life of Buddha and his teachings.

Dravidian   Pertaining to the indigenous race of people of south India and their languages. Primarily Tamil, Telegu, and Malayalam.

Dṛṣtivāda   One of the ancillary Jain sacred texts.

gandharas   The eleven principle disciples, the so-called "keepers of the host," of Mahavira Vardhamana, the founder of the established form of Jainism.

Ganeśa   The Hindu deity depicted with an elephant's head who is invoked at the beginning of every enterprise for its successful completion.

gōtra   The Hindu family clan.

grantha-bhāṇḍāra   Storehouse of books.

Hanumān   Hindu monkey-headed divinity, currently a common deity in central and upper India.

hiṃsā   Any act causing harm to living creatures.

Jātaka   Birth tale describing one of the former lives of Buddha.

jāti   The stratification system which most directly affects the daily lives of the Indian people. Traditionally, each varṇa was assigned a broad occupational field known as jāti. Thus, there are four varṇas, or castes proper, but many jātis.

Jina   "Victor"; one who has conquered his passions and obtained mastery over himself. Thus, the enlightened one. Jainism means the way to attain the state of becoming a Jina.

jīva   The vital force of life and consciousness which exists in all living creatures, according to Jainism.

Kalpa-sūtra   One of the primary texts of Jainism describing the lives of former Jinas and containing rules for monks.

kāma   Pleasure and the pleasure principle.

Kāma-sūtra   Genre of rule books describing the theory and practice of pleasure, primarily sexual pleasure.

karma   Act or action produced by or upon a living creature. The totality of such acts in one's lifetime determines one's future existence.

Kāvya   Intricate and bombastic classical poetry of India.

kevala   The pure and complete stage of enlightenment when consciousness exists in a person in an isolated state, free of any effects of actions. Such a state leads to liberation.

Kṣatriya   Any member of the ancient Indian ruling class. They were originally warriors.

Kural   Lyric Tamil text of South India.

Mahāparijñā   One of the ancillary Jain sacred texts.

Manu, Laws of   The oldest and most revered ancient Hindu Dharma-śastra (q.v.).

maṭha   An assembly hall, primarily utilized as a place of instruction and teaching.

māyā   The Hindu notion of illusion or deception as an active force which prevents people from realizing the true nature of existence.

mokṣa (moksha)   Release and freedom from the cycle of rebirths. This can only be attained by true enlightenment and victory over one's self and actions. It is the goal of every religious person.

Naladiyara   Lyric Tamil text of South India.

nirgantha   A term for the Jain ascetic monk. Originally, such monks were undraped, and thus received this title which means clothesless. See also Digambara.

nirjara The final step to liberation for the Jains. This occurs when the effects of actions fall away from persons and pure consciousness and intelligence only exist for them.

nirvāṇa The Buddhist concept of enlightenment. It occurs when all the effects which bring on rebirth are extinguished by understanding.

parameshthin One who has attained enlightenment and stands in the highest level of existence.

parigraha Principle of selfish attachment to objects and persons in this world.

Pārśvanātha (Parśva): According to tradition, the twenty-third Jain saint who lived in the 8th century B.C. He was the predecessor of Mahāvira Vardhamāna.

paryuṣaṇa Jain festival of ten days which celebrates the end of the rainy season.

pratikramaṇa Act of confession of Jains, much like the Catholic practice.

pūjari Temple priest who conducts the Jain sacred rites.

Purāna Genre of ancient Hindu text containing the repertory of traditional myths and legends.

rājā King.

sadhvī Class of female Jain ascetics, who organized communities like those of the monks.

saṃsāra The cycle of rebirths to which one is bound until he attains liberation.

samvatsari Final day of rainy season festival. It marks the transition point between years.

saṇkhyā System of ancient Hindu pilosophy.

sannyāsa The principle of total rejection and renunciation of worldly interests.

Shūdra Any member of the lowest or servant class in ancient India. Most of these were not Aryans but were comprised of the indigenous peoples of India conquered by the Aryan invaders.

Siddhārta   The king who was the father of Mahāvīra Vardamāna.

Skanda   Hindu deity.

srāvaka   Any member of the lay order of Jains.

Stānakavāsi   Independent sect of Jain monks.

sutee   Hindu practice of a wife burning herself on her husband's funeral pyre.

Sūtra   Genre of ancient Indian rule books for every field of inquiry.

Svetāmbara   One of the two principal Jain sects of monks. Their name derives from the fact that they wore white garments.

syādvāda   Jain philosophical theory of alternate existing possibilities out of which the total truth may be discerned.

Syādvāda-mañjari   Jain text which summarizes the theory of possibilities.

Tīrthaṇkara   Any of the Jain saints who have already attained liberation by "crossing the stream of (worldly) existence."

Tirthankara Prameshthin   One who has attained all but the final stage of liberation.

upāśraya   Jain assembly hall used for meetings and for instruction.

Vaiśya   Any member of the Hindu class of merchants and tradesmen.

vāṇija   Same as bāṇiya, q.v.

Vardhamāna Mahāvīra   The founder of the established form of Jainism.

varṇa   Literally, "color"; Sanskrit term for caste, from the Portuguese "casta," meaning "division." There are four main varṇas.

yoga   Ancient Hindu system of philosophy which teaches liberation through restraint and effort.

INDEX

Capitalists Without Capitalism was
composed in Intertype Garamond with Optima
display type and printed by offset lithography by
Port City Press, Inc., Baltimore, Maryland.
The book was bound by Arnold's Book
Bindery, Reading, Pennsylvania.